CRYSTALS FOR WITCHES

Interior and Cover Designer: Carlos Esparza
Art Producer: Hannah Dickerson
Editor: Carolyn Abate

Illustrations © 2020 Ameya Ajay. Photography © Lucia Loiso, p. 60; all other photogra-phy used under license from Shutterstock.com and iStock.com.

ISBN: Print 978-1-64611-080-3 | eBook 978-1-64611-081-0
Printed in Canada
R0

Crystals

FOR

Witches

RITUALS, SPELLS, AND PRACTICES FOR STONE-SPIRIT MAGIC

Eliza Mabelle

ILLUSTRATIONS BY

Ameya Ajay

ROCKRIDGE PRESS

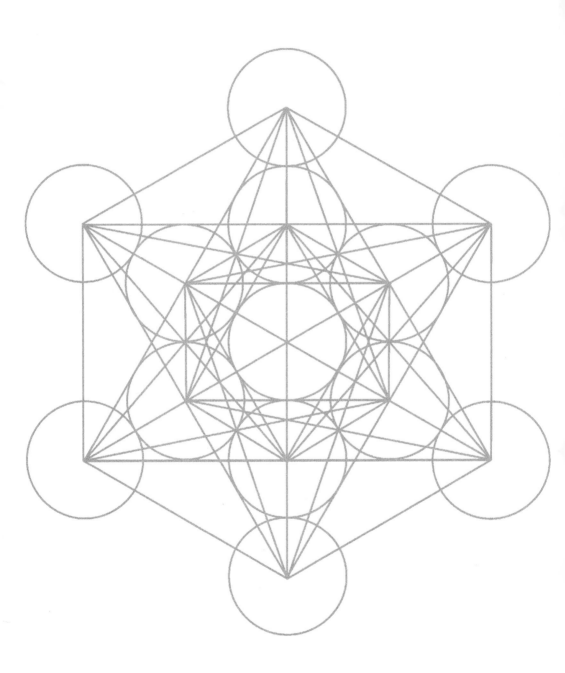

CONTENTS

INTRODUCTION VII

PART ONE: UNDERSTANDING STONE-SPIRIT MAGIC 1

Chapter One: The Power of Crystal Magic 3

Chapter Two: Working with Crystals 21

Chapter Three: Crystal Companions 39

30 Crystal Profiles 39

100 Additional Crystals to Know 70

PART TWO: 50 SPELLS, RITUALS, RITES, AND OTHER MAGICAL PRACTICES 89

Abundance and Prosperity 92

Protection and Clearing 99

Love and Relationships 107

Creativity and Manifestation 114

Divination and Spiritual Awakening 120

Self-Care and Emotional Healing 127

Physical Health and Wellness 135

Ceremonial Rites and Celebrations 142

RESOURCES 155

INDEX 157

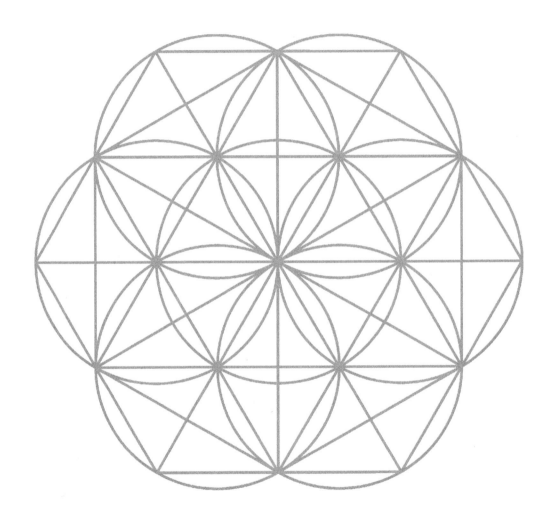

INTRODUCTION

In the midst of climate change and ecological crisis, people worldwide are gaining a better understanding of the importance of respecting the natural world. Many are awakening to the realization that a sacred spirit resides in everything in our universe, from the earth and trees to the wind and stars.

This emerging consciousness is manifesting in many ways, one of which is a surge in the popularity of crystals. Mainstream culture has stumbled upon something that seems new but is in fact as old as human history: the power of crystals. These colorful, sparkling nuggets of beauty hold a mystical allure, resonating with something magical inside almost all of us.

When it comes to earth-based spiritual practices such as witchcraft, there's an innate connection to all of nature's creations, including stones. Crystals are especially magical; they have the power to attract, repel, absorb, or affect energies in and around a person or situation. A stone's role in witchcraft is determined by its color, shape, history, and vibration, along with the personal relationship that develops between the witch and the spirit within the crystal.

The word *witchcraft* is a broad term, encompassing many kinds of practices and belief systems. Although it's true there are structured approaches to witchcraft, such as Wicca and other paths with initiation rites, you don't have to belong to a tradition or a bloodline or have a specific label to practice witchcraft. Witchcraft is intensely personal; it speaks from within your unique soul and heart.

My personal path into witchcraft has been solitary and intuitive, which means the things I've learned and practiced are nondenominational. This book is written with the same open spirit and can be used by anyone who is interested in witchcraft and crystals. If you're already a practicing witch, the information given here can be tweaked easily to suit your existing beliefs. If you're brand-new to witchcraft, this book presents some of the basics, with a particular focus on crystal magic.

Many witches have an animistic view of the world, believing that everything in nature has a spirit within it. Crystals are like supercharged clusters of this life-energy. As you learn how to integrate your crystal companions into your witchcraft practice, you will form unique relationships with them, the same way you may have a distinctive bond with certain animals or plants.

This book will teach you how to choose and source your crystals and see how they fit into your witchcraft practice. A large portion of the book is dedicated to identifying stones and listing their magical properties, to help you deepen your understanding of the crystal world. In part 2, there's a collection of spells and rituals for you to try, each invoking crystal magic in diverse ways.

I have a close relationship with several crystals as part of my witchcraft practice, and I often integrate them into my spells and rituals. For example, I've made money-attracting amulets using iron pyrite and created success candles with tumbled carnelian stones in the wax to boost their power. I've buried protective crystals around the perimeter of my property to keep it safe. These are all examples of how witchcraft and crystals can work together. This book will help you cultivate your personal witchcraft practice, with crystal companions by your side.

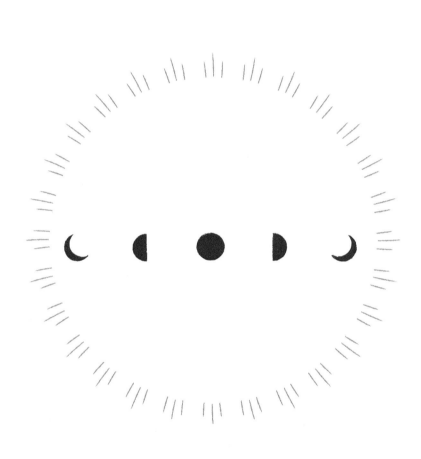

PART ONE

UNDERSTANDING STONE-SPIRIT MAGIC

When you first discover the worlds of crystals and witchcraft, there's an overwhelming amount of information, which can make it difficult to know where to begin. In part 1 of this book, we're starting with the absolute basics of crystal magic, focusing on how and why stone spirits are part of the witchcraft practice. This foundation will enable you to build your own personal relationship with stone spirits and guide you in welcoming them into your life.

CHAPTER ONE

THE POWER OF CRYSTAL MAGIC

Crystals, gems, and minerals are receptacles of powerful energy. They share the same life force as every plant, animal, an element in the cosmos. I call this energy *Spirit*. Spirit is the force that witches tap into to effect change in our lives and the world around us. Some witches consider Spirit to be the fifth element, alongside earth, air, fire, and water. In this chapter, you'll learn how stones and crystals are an integral part of the practice of witchcraft.

STONE OR SPIRIT?

Crystals have fascinated humans since the dawn of time, playing roles in both the scientific and spiritual worlds. Some view crystals as purely material things that are pretty to look at, whereas others believe they possess magical powers that cannot be explained. These seemingly opposite views meet when you put crystals and witchcraft together. We recognize their beauty, but we also believe they house Spirit energy.

Crystal Science

Every crystal is made of a fixed, microscopic pattern of atoms, molecules, and ions that, when left undisturbed, will continuously repeat and extend outward in a predictable and never-changing lattice structure. The crystal's ability to hold, channel, and manipulate energy is directly connected to its infinitely continuous lattice structure, which forms facets, planes, cubes, hexagons, and other shapes.

Crystals are used in modern technology to conduct energy, and some possess a detectible electromagnetic field that affects the human body. Quartz crystals have a quality called piezoelectricity, which means they can produce electricity when they are compressed. Quartz crystal carries an electrical charge at a sustained, constant frequency, which is why it's an important part of radios, computers, watches, and other devices. This ability extends from physics to metaphysics; since crystals are known to generate and conduct natural forces, it's also believed they can harness and manipulate personal forces such as emotions and intentions as well as healing energy. Energy healers draw upon the unique vibrations emitted from various crystals to treat ailments by adding, removing, and balancing the energy within the body.

There's a lot of terminology that gets mixed up when talking about crystals. The terms *crystal*, *stone*, *mineral*, and *gem* are often used interchangeably, but they actually refer to different things.

CRYSTAL: A crystal occurs when a microscopic combination of atoms, molecules, and ions forms a set pattern that continuously and perfectly repeats itself, creating a three-dimensional geometric form that appears as points, faceted planes, and angles. Crystals may form from minerals, but they can also form from organic substances. (Sugar and proteins are two examples of organic crystals.) Unlike rocks, crystals do not contain more than one material.

MINERAL: A mineral is formed deep in the earth. Each mineral has a specific chemical composition and an internal crystalline structure. They are naturally occurring, solid, and don't contain any fossilized organic materials from plants or animals. Minerals form as a result of heat, pressure, or the evaporation of moisture within the earth. It can take thousands or millions of years for crystals to form from minerals. They require precise environmental conditions that vary from mineral to mineral. Two minerals can actually have the same chemical composition and yet completely different crystal structures.

ROCK OR STONE: Rocks are made from many minerals, mineraloids (a naturally occurring mineral-like substance that does not have a crystalline structure), and organic material mixed together, including fossilized vegetation and animals. Some stones that are called crystals are technically rocks, like lapis lazuli and jade.

GEMSTONES: A gemstone is a precious or semiprecious stone that's hard enough to be cut into jewelry. Gemstones may be crystals, minerals, rocks, or even organic materials such as amber.

For the sake of simplicity, I'll be using the terms *crystal*, *stone*, and *gem* interchangeably throughout this book. I'll also talk about other precious substances, such as amber and pearls, which aren't crystals. However, these materials are naturally formed, possess ancient power, and can be integrated into your witchcraft just like crystals, gems, and stones.

Energy and Spirit

The best-known spiritual use of crystals is in energy healing, such as Reiki and chakra therapy. It's believed that different crystals resonate with the different energy centers in our physical and spiritual bodies, helping to align, clear, or repair them. Some energy healers believe crystals can also relieve health conditions like high blood pressure, intestinal problems, and headaches.

In these practices, crystals act as a conduit for sending concentrated healing power where it's needed. When it comes to witchcraft, we take this a step further, believing that a crystal can also affect the world around us by attracting or repelling forces outside of ourselves, such as love, abundance, and protection.

CRYSTALS FOR WITCHES

A witch's relationship with crystals is similar to the relationship they have with other animate or living things. Much like an animal or plant, each stone has a distinct vibration or spirit residing within it. Different crystals are associated with different magical properties, such as attracting friendship, inspiring courage, or warding off negativity. Witches include crystals in spells, rituals, and meditations based on these qualities. Gemstones are also an important component in many witchcraft practices and are regarded with respect and love.

Gifts from Mother Nature

Witchcraft is rooted in a bond with nature. Many witches recognize the spirit that lives within all natural things, from wind to fire, trees to rain. Although all rocks, even ordinary ones, are considered powerful in their own way, crystals are special. Crystals are formed when a specific combination of natural phenomena occurs within the earth, such as heat, pressure, and water movement. This imbues them with far different energy than a common pebble has. For example, obsidian is formed when molten lava meets water, which grants it very special properties. Their beauty, rarity, and the unique conditions needed for their creation make crystals cherished gifts from Mother Nature.

Crystal Magic

Many people are intuitively attracted to the energy or spirit of crystals. With practice and patience, you can learn to feel and interact with these forces to enhance your spells and rituals. Meditation and intention are the first steps toward successfully working with stone spirits.

Meditation quiets the mind and puts you in a calm, receptive state. Crystals, like many natural beings, have a subtle way of communicating that you have to be in the right frame of mind to experience. A distracted or stressed person will have difficulty interacting with the spirit of a stone.

To understand your crystals, do some deep-breathing exercises and enter a relaxed, open mindset. Hold the crystal in your hand and allow feelings and impressions to flow. You might be able to feel a subtle vibration surrounding the stone, or even see an aura or energy field. While in this meditative state, pay attention to how you feel. Some crystals create feelings of peace, whereas others have an energizing effect. This exercise will tell you a lot about the properties of that particular stone.

Once you have achieved this understanding of a particular crystal, you can set your intention. Aligning your intention with the energy of the crystal is much like taking the existing power within the spirit of the stone and channeling it in a certain direction. Your intention, whether it's to attract love, bring protection, or something else, must be clear and concise. A crystal is powerful on its own, but it needs to be aligned with your desired outcome to manifest your plans. It's helpful if your goals match the magical properties of the stone, so having a basic understanding of the attributes of different crystals is useful. (You'll find more information about that in chapter 3.)

PRACTICING THE CRAFT YOUR WAY

If you're a practicing witch with your own established belief system, crystal magic can merge seamlessly into your current beliefs, bringing a new dimension to your practice. Crystals can be part of your witchcraft the same way you include other elements, such as herbs and other plants. Like herbs, stones are chosen for spells and rituals based on their magical properties. You can place crystals on your altar to attract magical energy or enhance the results of spells, add them to your meditation routine, or make them into amulets without changing your methods.

You may find that crystals formed in parts of the world connected to your tradition are especially meaningful to you. If there are specific gods, goddesses, or deities you have a connection with, crystals can be dedicated to them as an offering. You might even find that specific stones resonate with the character traits of certain deities.

Integrating stone magic into your witchcraft should in no way change or interfere with your current practice. If you're drawn to them, you'll find that crystals only enrich and add a new type of energy and power to your witchcraft.

SACRED WORKSPACE

When you decide to begin your journey into crystal magic, it can be helpful to set up a special spot just for this purpose. In witchcraft, this sacred space is sometimes called an altar. A sacred space is useful for several reasons. It signals to your subconscious mind that you've entered a spiritual realm, which helps create the right mindset to commune with your crystals. It will show respect to your crystal companions by giving them their own place of honor, and over time an energetic imprint will form in this spot; the more time you spend practicing there, the more peaceful and powerful it will be.

A sacred space or altar doesn't have to be large or elaborate. It can be as simple as an end table or even a windowsill. You'll need a flat surface to work on if you plan to do spells, grids, or rituals. Choose an area where you won't be disturbed by others, and where you're comfortable turning off your electronic devices and being in the now. Be sure it's a spot that feels calm to you; avoid places where something distressing has recently occurred.

If you already have an altar, you can work with your crystals on it as you would any other magical material.

Magical Items and Tools

Here are some items you may wish to include in your sacred space.

THE ELEMENTS: Often in witchcraft, the four elements of earth, air, fire, and water are invoked during spells and rituals. Some witches include the fifth element of Spirit; depending on their practice, this can also be referred to as chosen gods or goddesses, the universe, or the All. Consider having an object to represent each of these on your altar, such as a seashell for water, a feather for air, a plant for earth, and a small candle for fire. Spirit can be represented by a statue, a crystal tower, or a white candle.

INCENSE: Stick or cone incense, with its scent and the visual beauty of smoke, can be helpful in bringing about a meditative state of mind. Incense smoke can also be used to cleanse crystals. Some people prefer to use loose, natural incense that must be burned on a charcoal disk in a heatproof dish.

TRAY: Find a tray, preferably made of an organic material such as wood, that will only be used to put your crystals on when you give them a moon bath. It can be large or small, depending on how many crystals you will place on it.

CANDLES: Candlelight creates a peaceful, glowing light that is perfect for helping you reach the mental state you need to work with crystals. It also declares to Spirit that you're doing sacred work.

SMALL BAGS: Small cloth or leather drawstring bags can be useful for carrying more than one crystal with you at a time.

SELENITE WAND: Selenite is believed to simultaneously cleanse and empower all the other crystals it touches, so it's very useful to have some.

PENTACLE DISK: The pentacle, a five-pointed star in a circle, is a sacred symbol in witchcraft. The lower points of the star represent the elements of earth, air, fire, and water, and the uppermost point represents Spirit. The circle reflects the never-ending cycle of rebirth. You may wish to have a pentacle disk on your altar made of wood, metal, or cloth.

CLEANSING SMOKE OR SPRAY: Some people wish to cleanse their sacred space every time they enter it, with either a spray of water and essential oils or smoke from burning dried plants chosen for their magical properties, such as sage. Spreading the mist or smoke around the space clears away unwanted accumulated energy from everyday life.

JOURNAL: Set aside a small journal just for your sacred work with crystals. As you learn about different crystals, write down your impressions in the journal. Doing so will help you remember which stones resonate with you and how they might be included later in rituals.

ETHICAL MINING, FAIR TRADE, AND OTHER SOURCING CONSIDERATIONS

The environmental and ethical impact of mining healing stones weighs heavily on a lot of people's minds. There are questions and concerns about the impact on the Earth, the well-being of workers, and the true cost of crystals in the big picture. Here are some things to keep in mind when sourcing your stones.

- **Do your research.** When shopping, seek out vendors who are transparent and have a clear mission statement about ethically sourced crystals. Many stone sellers are concerned about these issues as well and will be happy to share this information.
- **Think geographically.** Crystals that are mined in countries where working conditions are strictly regulated are less likely to contribute to worker exploitation. Find out where in the world a crystal comes from, so you can research the working conditions surrounding its excavation.
- **Value your crystals.** Even though some crystals are inexpensive, they aren't single-use items. Remember, crystals can take millions of years to form naturally. Rather than buying a new rose quartz every time you want to cast a love spell, cleanse the rose quartz you have and reuse it. Cleansing can be done with all crystals.
- **Raise your voice.** Remember that the more customers like you demand ethical mining and fair trade, the more businesses will have to comply. Take a stand with your dollars.

YOUR CRYSTAL COMPANIONS

Discovering crystal companions and learning how to integrate them into your witchcraft is a mystical but also fun experience. Here are some ways to make these new relationships as positive as possible.

Finding Your Crystals

Crystals are currently so popular that you can find them almost anywhere: in malls, at large retailers, and in home decor stores. Typically, the best way to find crystals is in shops that sell items for metaphysical uses (in person or online) or by attending gem shows and expos. At these events, you can speak to knowledgeable people about your purchases and gain deeper insight into your gems as well as find out how they were sourced.

Ideally, you'll purchase your crystals in person so you can touch them and get a sense of their energy—although online shopping has some perks, including access to a wider variety of stones and vendors. When browsing crystals, you'll notice certain gems catch your eye more than others. If you're drawn to a stone again and again for any reason at all, such as color, shape, or a certain something you can't even name, that crystal is calling out to you. The same can be said for online shopping: If it's grabbing your attention visually, or if it's associated with a person or place that's meaningful to you, there's a good chance it's destined to be with you.

When possible, hold the crystal in your hand and try to feel its energy. A stone that aligns well with you may give off a slight vibration, a tingling sensation, or an impression of warmth or coolness. If the crystal feels oppressive, unpleasant in your hand, or just empty, it's not for you at this time. Sometimes a crystal will feel wrong or off simply because it isn't the one you need in your life right now, and you're being directed away from it toward a more suitable stone.

If at any time a crystal comes to you by chance, whether as a gift or a random find at a garage sale, that crystal is absolutely meant for you and has sought you out for a reason.

Healing and Connecting with Crystals

If you handle a crystal you're drawn to and discover that it feels off, especially if you bought it online, it may be because its energy field has been damaged on its journey to you. A crystal that has been handled by many people can absorb the emotions of each individual. If it was taken disrespectfully from the earth or was mined in a way that was hurtful to people and the ecosystem, this crystal may need healing before you can work with it. The same is true for a crystal that's been heavily used for healing purposes. Think of it as tending to an animal or plant that needs to be nurtured back to health. Don't try to do any spells or rituals with it for now; rather, let it rest and show it some care. Here are some things you can do.

- Place the crystal in the earth and allow it to stabilize for several days. Imagine the earth is absorbing all the negative energy from the crystal and grounding it.

- Leave the crystal in a warm, sunny spot and imagine it soaking up the comforting rays.

- Carry it with you where it can absorb the heat of your body along with your healing intentions.

- Sleep with it under your pillow, where it will continue to benefit from the energy you are sending it.

- Exhale onto the crystal and imagine your breath is a soft, warm, healing mist. You are sending your own vitality and life-energy into the crystal. Repeat several times a day.

After trying these things, hold the crystal in your hand and try to feel whether it has improved. It may take several attempts to completely clear or heal a crystal. Cleansing the crystal, as I'll explain later in this chapter, may also be helpful in the healing process.

If after doing all of this you're still uncomfortable with the stone, give it away or return it to the earth and let it go.

A witch can maintain a strong, healthy connection with their crystal companions simply by remembering to be aware of them. Just briefly handling a stone is acknowledging it and therefore empowering it. Occasionally spend some time touching them one by one and feeling the difference between each of them. This is a kind of check-in with your magical stones and the Spirit energy within them.

Remember to listen to your crystals: Sometimes one will demand your attention by dropping on the floor or otherwise catching your eye. Carry it with you for some time or keep it near during meditation. It either has something to tell you, or you simply need its unique energy with you that day. If one of your crystals seems to be calling out to you, try sleeping with it near your bed or under your pillow and a message may come to you in a dream.

Cleansing and Care

Crystals pick up on the energy around them and sometimes hold on to it. If a crystal is used regularly for healing, it will absorb some of the vibrations from that experience. Crystals that have been passed around to lots of people or left unused for a length of time will also need to be cleared of accumulated energy. Think of cleansing your crystals as hitting a reset button. After being cleansed, a crystal's energy vibrates clear and true. Here are some ways to cleanse your crystals.

WATER BATH: Place the crystal in a bowl of water. Allow the stone to sit for several hours, letting the water gently pull away and absorb the accumulated energy. After this clarifying bath, let the crystal air dry and dispose of the water. Keep in mind, though, that some stones can be damaged by water. This information is included in the individual crystal profiles in chapter 3.

SMOKE CLEANSING: Pass the crystals through smoke from incense or burning herbs. Hold the crystal in the stream of smoke while visualizing its energy field becoming clear and bright. If you're burning your own dried herbs, you can choose purifying ones, such as bay leaves or rosemary. Burning a sage bundle is a ceremony sacred to some Native American and Indigenous peoples known as smudging. While increasingly popular, smudging is a meaningful ritual in Native and Indigenous culture, so if you choose to smudge, make sure you're being respectful of their traditions and mindful of where you source your sage.

SALT: Salt cleanses and heals in many practical ways, and the same properties can be applied to crystals. Bury your crystal in a dish of sea salt, covering it completely. Let it sit for several hours. The salt will absorb unwanted vibrations from the crystal. Some people like to mix water and sea salt for their crystal bath. Remember that salt is corrosive to some crystals and might ruin them. This information is provided in chapter 3.

NATURAL WATER SOURCES: If it's raining, consider placing water-safe crystals outdoors during the shower. Rain is nature's cleanser. You can also find a gentle unpolluted stream or other body of water and let your crystals sit in it for a few hours, so long as the current will not whisk them away.

SELENITE: Selenite is a gypsum mineral that cleanses and empowers all crystals that come in contact with it. Place your crystal so it's touching the selenite and leave it overnight. Selenite will draw out unwanted energy and neutralize it, while simultaneously recharging the crystal.

SNOW: If you live in a cold climate, place your crystal in a container and cover it with clean snow. Bring it indoors to melt. As the snow changes from ice crystals into water, it transforms the energy of the crystal to its purest state. Don't do this with crystals that can be damaged by water.

There are a few things you can do to keep the energy of your crystals healthy and clear between cleansings. Be sure to wrap brittle or delicate stones in individual pieces of soft cloth to keep them whole and safe. Give your crystals their own special box or bowl when you're not using them to protect them from outside vibrations and dust. Place a chunk of selenite in the box to keep them cleansed and protected. During the full moon, place them outdoors or on a windowsill to absorb the lunar energy.

Taking physical care of your stones by keeping them clean and protected from damage goes a long way toward keeping your relationship with their Spirit energy positive and powerful. Remember that you have a bond with your crystals, and you should interact with them even when you're not actively trying to manifest something. Acknowledging their power only when you need them to do "work" and ignoring them otherwise is disrespectful.

Charging

Charging a crystal is a key part of integrating it into your witchcraft. Think of it like charging your phone; neglect to do it long enough and its power will go dormant. Crystals, when undisturbed or unused for lengths of time, have the same reaction. Your stones need to be charged with power from the natural world. Doing so feeds them, in a sense, keeping their energy fresh and revived. Here are some basic techniques for charging your crystal companions.

QUARTZ POINTS: Place the crystal that needs charging on a flat surface and surround it with three or more quartz crystals, with the points facing inward. Quartz directs and amplifies energy, so aiming it at your stone channels positive energy right into it.

SUNLIGHT: Sunlight is another natural way to charge crystals. The sun makes plants grow and life flourish. Set your stones in direct sunlight for several hours and visualize that fertile energy being absorbed by the crystal, awakening it like a blooming flower. Some crystals can fade in prolonged sunlight, which may affect their magical power. To avoid fading, shorten the time they're left in the sun to just a few minutes. (This information is included in the individual crystal profiles in chapter 3.)

MOONLIGHT: The full moon is also an important source for charging. Place your crystals either outdoors or on a windowsill. Even if it's a cloudy night, the energy of the moon will find them and fill them with power.

VISUALIZATION: Enter a relaxed, meditative state. Become aware of the energy in your heart center, how it beats and throbs with the rhythm of life. Imagine white light coming from your chest. Hold the crystal to your chest and envision your heart energy completely surrounding and saturating the crystal, throbbing life into the stone. Maintain this image for as long as you can.

PENTACLE: If you have an altar, place your crystal in the center of a pentacle disk. You can also draw a pentacle on paper or cloth and use it the same way. If you're experienced in creating your own sigils or symbols, you can design them to charge crystals.

CANDLES: Light six or more white candles in a small circle on your magic work area, altar, or sacred space. Place your crystal in the center and light the candles. Allow the vibrant fire energy to infuse the stone. Blow, pinch, or snuff out the candles when you're finished.

PLANTS: Place the crystal at the foot of a healthy tree where it can touch the roots or bark. You could also place the crystal in a potted plant where it can connect with the pure vitality of a growing, living thing.

HERBS: Mugwort is an herb used in witchcraft to increase psychic powers. It's often used to charge tools used in magic. You can boil a bit of dried mugwort into a tea, let it cool, and place the crystal in it for several hours. You can also keep some dried mugwort in a container and place the crystal in it, covering it completely and letting it sit for several hours. Other herbs that are good for charging crystals include rose petals, rosemary, and sage.

Empowering

Empowering a crystal is different from charging it. The cleansed and charged crystal itself is powerful and full of energy, but that energy needs to be given direction. Empowering, or programming as it's sometimes called, is a means of giving the crystal a specific task to aid in manifesting a desired outcome. There are many different purposes that can be allotted to crystals, such as attracting love or abundance, creating an energetically protective barrier, and increasing psychic awareness. Be sure you have clearly decided upon your intention before you begin.

1. Cleanse and charge your crystal.

2. In your sacred space or at your altar, light a candle and do some deep breathing to ground and center yourself.

3. Hold the crystal in your hand. Be aware of the aura, vibration, or energetic field around it. Notice how you share the same energy field as the crystal—the humming life force of all living things.

4. State your intention out loud or whisper it to the crystal. Some people find it helpful to chant an intention over and over in order to raise energy. You can state the crystal's purpose in one sentence, for example: *I empower you to instill me with courage* or *I empower you to create a peaceful environment.*

5. Visualize your goal as if you already have it. Don't devote this time to worrying about how you will achieve your goal, but rather trust Spirit to manifest your desire in the most positive way possible, picturing the outcome exactly as you'd like it to be. This kind of focused visualization is the most important aspect of spell casting and empowering your crystal. Allow yourself to feel and experience in your mind obtaining your wish.

6. Visualize that your goal, the mental images you created, and the emotions you felt are inside a bubble of light in front of your face. Visualize this bubble of powerful intention settling over the crystal and filling it completely.

7. Now your crystal is programmed, or empowered, to attract the very thing you have visualized.

8. Carry the crystal with you or use it in your magic as you wish. Every time you see or touch the crystal, you will feel the power of your intention.

Once you have cleansed, charged, and empowered a crystal, you have a powerful ally. The crystal vibrates with the same frequency as the entire natural world and the universe, and has now been filled with your own intentions and visions. The crystal is sending out a signal to the universe that bears the vision of your goal. Every time you charge your crystal in any of the methods described, it will strengthen the power and intention you have put into it.

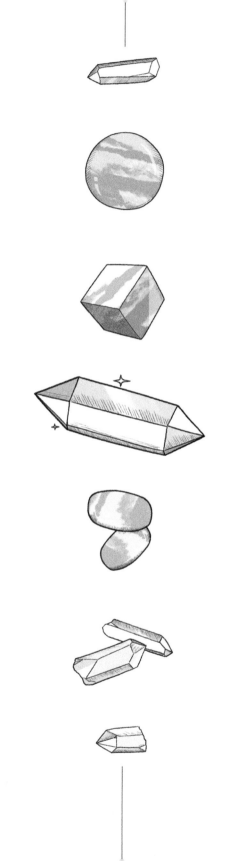

CHAPTER TWO

WORKING WITH CRYSTALS

Now that you've begun to explore stone-spirit magic, we'll look deeper into the many ways witches integrate crystals into spells, rituals, and divination. The physical appearance of a crystal affects its purpose, as does how you choose to use it—whether it's as an altar decoration, as an amulet to keep with your tarot cards, or as part of a crystal grid.

DIFFERENT ATTRIBUTES FOR DIFFERENT NEEDS

Beyond being visually or intuitively drawn to a certain stone, there are other factors to consider when choosing a crystal to include in your witchcraft. Shape, size, and color will all come into play. These variables have universal meanings but can also have psychological associations that will affect how you interact with a stone.

Sizes

When it comes to crystals, size doesn't matter as long as your intention is strong. A tiny bead of malachite can pack the same wallop as a large chunk. Size is really about preference and practicality. Sometimes you'll want a larger crystal to place in a spot that is important, such as an altar, as a constant source of energy. Sometimes you'll need a smaller stone that's more versatile and portable.

Fortunately, crystals come in all sizes, from as tiny as pebbles to as large as furniture! Stones that fit in your hand are the perfect size for personal use. In witchcraft, your own energy and intention are fused with the crystal, and this relationship is far more important and powerful than size.

Colors

Color magic is often one of the first things a witch learns about on their path. Each color on the spectrum has specific energies and powers, which is why the color of candles and other tools is important in spellwork. The color of a crystal plays a big role in determining its magical properties and how it affects you psychologically and spiritually.

Crystals and stones that have similar hues very often share magical properties. However, just as every color comes in almost endless shades and tones, each stone's energy is different. For example, moss agate and aventurine both come in shades of green, which is the color of growth and abundance. However, moss agate emphasizes the growth of physical health and stamina, whereas green aventurine is associated with creativity and imagination.

They both share the symbolism of growth because of their color, yet the type of growth is different.

Here are some of the basic color meanings in witchcraft; you may find they explain why you are drawn to some stones over others.

RED: passion, courage, sex, boldness, determination

PINK: love, friendship, emotional connection, gentleness

ORANGE: success, triumph, strength, power

YELLOW: joy, warmth, independence, creativity, confidence

GREEN: growth, abundance, prosperity, fertility, luck

BLUE: healing, communication, sending messages, intellect, empathy

PURPLE: psychic ability, occult power, intuition, universal truth, wisdom

BROWN: connection to animals, comfort, the home, physical rest

BLACK: protection, grounding, shielding, introspection

WHITE: healing, spirituality, connection to the higher self or spirit world

CLEAR: clarity of mind, body, and spirit; purification; vision; amplification of intention

GRAY: peace, calm, settling chaotic energy

Shapes

The shape of a stone affects the crystal's vibration itself, and also how you connect with it. For example, a smooth, heart-shaped stone evokes different feelings than a rough, jagged shard. The shape will also have an impact on your magical working.

POINT: A crystal that's naturally pointed can be used to direct energy away from or toward something. To amplify the power of an amulet, aim a quartz point at it during empowerment. To strengthen a spell, have a point facing outward to send the power into the world.

Points are sometimes natural and sometimes hand-carved; both can serve the same purpose.

CLUSTER: Many crystals grow in a cluster, which looks like a collection of points forming a spiky mass. This natural bloom of crystal is a powerful conduit for the energy of the stone, radiating its power out into the world through the points.

RAW: Raw stones are in their natural state, as they were taken straight from the earth, and have not been polished, tumbled, or cut. Raw stones have had minimal human interaction and therefore some believe they possess a higher vibration; however, this is a subjective opinion. You will have to see if it rings true for you.

WORRY STONE: These are cut into small, smooth oval disks that are perfect for rubbing between your fingers. The purpose of a worry stone is to sooth anxiety while absorbing and grounding chaotic energy.

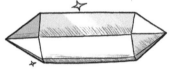

DOUBLE POINT: A point on both ends of a crystal can send energy in two directions at once, making it perfect to include in spells for balance and equilibrium.

HEART: Smooth, heart-shaped crystals are always popular for a variety of reasons. They can enhance spells for love in all its forms, whether it's romantic, familial, friendship, or self-love. They can also be carried to heal a broken heart.

SPHERE: A crystal ball is often mentioned in scrying and divination. This is typically done with quartz or other translucent crystals, but can also be achieved with dark, shiny stones like obsidian or hematite. A crystal sphere is a symbol of the interconnectedness of all things, the never-ending circle that is life, death, and rebirth. The perfectly round shape of a crystal ball ensures that the energy it emits is evenly spread all around it.

WAND: Crystal wands come in many sizes and styles. Wands are cut into long, straight shapes with pointed or rounded ends and are used to direct energy in magic. A wand that comes to a tapered point is meant to gather the energy of that crystal and project it outward like a laser. A rounded wand is used for healing on the body in some holistic health practices.

OVAL: Oval palm stones are cut into just the right size and shape for holding in the hand and meditating. Depending on the properties of the crystal, you can hold a palm stone for grounding and relaxation, for clarity of mind, for increasing your own energy, and more.

PYRAMID: The shape of the pyramid appears in spiritual systems around the world. A pyramid is believed to draw upon the power of Spirit through its uppermost point and bring it down into the earthly realm in material form. When a crystal is cut like a pyramid, it intensifies its magical properties.

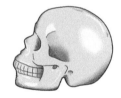

EGG: The symbolism of the egg is fertility, new beginnings, potential, and rebirth. Combining the egg shape with the properties of a crystal represents new beginnings in a specific area of life.

SKULL: Crystal skulls are often used for protection because the skull is a well-known symbol of warning. The crystal skull is also used in necromancy or contacting the dead, acting as a channel of communication between this world and the spirit world.

CUBE: A cube is a stabilizing shape. The cube will solidly hold the intention of your working, anchoring the energy of that intention in place.

WORKING WITH CRYSTALS

There are many ways witches integrate their crystal companions in their workings, spells, and rituals. Here's a summary of some common practices, which I'll be discussing in greater detail in part 2.

Wearing Crystals

When a witch wears a crystal, it's not just for aesthetics. Crystal necklaces, bracelets, and rings are usually magical amulets in the form of jewelry. And any form is fine. Crystals can be carved into bangles, strung as beads, or even embedded into metal—whatever makes the crystal easier to wear.

NECKLACES: A crystal or small bag of stones can be worn around your neck to attract various things into your life. Where the necklace hangs on your body is important and it can be adjusted by altering the length of the cord or chain. Wear a crystal necklace centered over your heart for spells involving emotions, love, and gratitude. A stone worn high on the throat as a choker is ideal for spells influencing communication and self-expression. You can wear a very long chain that places the crystal over your solar plexus center for inner strength and personal power.

RINGS: A ring placed on the index finger of your dominant hand (the hand you write with) can be a way of directing energy outward. To attract energy, wear it on your receiving hand (the hand you don't write with). If you wish to create healing energy, adorn your fingers with healing stones. The same is true for creating a kind touch, a loving touch, or a protective touch. Choose and wear your crystal rings according to what you wish to send or receive.

BRACELETS: To send energy outward, wear an appropriate crystal bracelet on your dominant arm. To attract something, wear a crystal bracelet on your non-dominant arm.

EARRINGS: When seeking guidance and illumination, wearing the appropriate crystal as earrings can help you receive messages, signs, and intuitive guidance.

ANKLETS: Wear anklets of a specific stone to symbolically guide your feet on a desired path or direction you want your life to go.

Altar Crystals

A witch's altar is a place for sacred, meaningful objects and will usually reflect what the witch is personally experiencing or working on at any point in their life. For this reason, you'll often find a variety of crystals there.

When choosing a crystal to place on your altar, be mindful that you'll be seeing it and interacting with it regularly. Aesthetics are important to some witches, and often they'll choose larger or showier stones for this place of honor. But, remember, smaller stones are just as magical.

Many witches' altars have items placed in the four cardinal directions to represent the elements of earth, air, fire, and water, along with something for the fifth element of Spirit. Below are the correspondences for these elements and some suggestions for crystals to represent each on an altar.

- North rules the element of earth. Earth represents stability, wealth, safety, protection, growth, and health. Some crystals and stones that align with elemental earth are petrified wood, unakite, green or brown jasper, and agate.

- East rules the element of air. Air encompasses communication, intellect, travel, and sending messages. Some crystals that align with elemental air are aventurine, opal, and sodalite.

- South rules the element of fire. Fire encompasses passion, transformation, change, and power. Crystals that align with elemental fire are ruby, garnet, carnelian, and sunstone.

- West rules the element of water. Water encompasses emotions, intuition, psychic ability, and purification. Crystals that align with elemental water are aquamarine, moonstone, and lapis lazuli.

- Spirit doesn't have a cardinal direction, and sometimes takes a place of honor at the center of an altar. Spirit represents the cycle of life, magical power, invisible forces, the souls of the dead, and fate. Crystals that align with Spirit are selenite, clear quartz, and howlite.

Crystal Tools

Many tools in witchcraft can be found or made with crystals integrated into them. Crystals can amplify the power of a witch's tools, add beauty to sacred objects, and attract desired energy into a magical item.

WANDS: A wand for directing energy, made of wood or metal, can have a crystal point on its tip for focusing energy. Or the design of the wand may be inlaid with various crystals chosen for their magical properties.

ATHAME: An athame is a traditional ritual knife that is sometimes carved from crystal or obsidian. While the double-edged ritual knife isn't meant to actually cut anything in the physical world and is often kept dull, it's used in rituals for creating barriers, channeling energy, and cutting energetic ties. The athame represents the active polarity in nature, such as growth, victory, dynamic change, and physical action.

CHALICE: The chalice is a goblet used for making offerings during rituals. They are often inlaid with crystals and gems to mark them as sacred vessels, used only in witchcraft rites, thus differentiating them from everyday drinking glasses. The chalice represents the receptive polarity in nature, which encompasses our inner worlds, psychic abilities, creativity, and thought.

SCRYING MIRROR: A scrying mirror is a divination tool sometimes made from black obsidian. You can gaze into the obsidian mirror as you would a crystal ball, and receive images and messages in answer to questions.

PENDULUM: A pendulum is a small object suspended on a chain or string, used in divination and dousing. Crystals make excellent pendulums because they carry electromagnetic energy.

AMULET: An amulet is a magical object witches carry with them, empowered with a certain task such as protection or attracting wealth. Crystals are perfect for amulets because they have preexisting properties, retain power, and can be made into jewelry for easy transport.

SACHET: Small or crushed crystal pieces can be added to a magical sachet, which is a collection of herbs and plants bundled into a small piece of cloth and tied closed. They are placed throughout the home or carried on a witch's person to attract and repel certain things, such as attracting friendship or repelling gossip.

OILS AND BREWS: Witches may blend essential oils or simmer herbs in water to create brews for use in spells. Oils and brews can be added to bathwater (assuming the ingredients are nontoxic), used for cleansing ritual objects, or dabbed onto the body to attract specific energies. Crystals are often added to these liquids to strengthen their magical power.

Crystal Grids

Crystals and stones laid out in a specific pattern with focused intent is known as a crystal grid. The crystals' proximity and the pattern of the grid enhances their power and helps them work together to manifest a goal. The shape of the grid is usually based on patterns that are found repeatedly in nature and throughout the universe—called sacred geometry.

A crystal grid is useful to witches because it enables us to combine the power of our crystals with ancient shapes and patterns that already hold great power. Since many sacred geometry patterns are quite complicated, you might want to buy a printed grid from a metaphysical store or print a free template from an online site. There are examples of some grids later on in part 2.

Your crystal grid should comprise stones that complement one another. Think of the crystals on your grid as a team, each bringing their own unique power to your magic and working toward a shared goal. Typically, a crystal grid includes a Master Stone, Way Stones, and Desire Stones. The Master Stone holds your intention, drawing energy from Spirit into itself. The stones that surround your Master Stone are called Way Stones. They amplify the energy of your Master Stone. Way Stones are usually quartz points to conduct energy. The outermost stones on a crystal grid are Desire Stones. They are chosen for their magical properties, according to what you wish to manifest. The number of Way and Desire Stones you will use depends on the grid itself.

Set up your crystal grid somewhere it won't be disturbed by pets or other people. It can be small enough to fit on your nightstand, as large as the perimeter of your home, or anything in between. Be sure to use crystals that have been cleansed and charged, and while creating your grid, focus clearly on your intention to empower the crystals.

The lines of the geometric shape of the grid conduct energy from your Master Stone, through the Way Stones, out through the Desire Stones—or the other way around, depending on what you are trying to achieve. Your intention gains energy as it flows along the lines of the sacred geometric shape, through the crystals, and into the universe. Use the following steps to set up your crystal grid:

1. Place your Master Stone in the center of the grid. Whisper your intention to the stone or write it on a slip of paper that you put beneath it.

2. Place the Way Stones around it on the intersecting lines of the grid.

3. Put your Desire Stones around the perimeter of the grid.

4. Take a quartz point, wand, or athame and trace the lines of the sacred geometric shape you have chosen, from one crystal to another, until you have worked your way to the center of the image. This act connects the stones energetically and aligns them with the sacred geometry of the universe. Your crystal grid is activated and complete.

A crystal grid can be made to attract things such as love, security, or harmony. It can be created to bring protection, to cleanse a space, or to anchor energy in one area. Every time you see your crystal grid, it reinforces your intention because it brings your goals to mind. You may be able to feel the vibrational push or pull around it.

Rituals and Spells

Including crystals in spells and rituals comes naturally to witches; there is a kind of added energetic push that only these amazing stones can deliver. They can invoke powerful feelings and energy when you touch them, and these stones enhance your alignment with the spell or working. Based on the spell they are casting, a witch may choose to adorn themself or their altar with specific crystals: wealth crystals for prosperity work, protection crystals for banishing, psychic-enhancement crystals for divination, and so on. Involving a well-loved crystal in a spell or ritual is like including an old friend who shares your vision. Your crystals know you as well as you know them!

When choosing a stone to incorporate into a spell or ritual, be sure to first cleanse, charge, and empower it with intention. Make sure the stone you've chosen resonates in a way that aligns with your goal by checking reference guides (including this one), and be sure to spend time getting to know your stone beforehand, as described in chapter 1.

To give your spell crystals an added boost, try sleeping with them under your pillow the night before your spell or working. Or simply carry them with you for a day, touching them occasionally. They'll absorb your thoughts and desires, and your ritual will be all the more powerful because of it.

Ceremonial Rites and Celebrations

Some witches observe eight traditional celebrations throughout the year. Each of these celebrations, sometimes called Sabbats, occur at significant times in the earth's travels around the sun, marking the changing seasons and nature's cycle. Together, these eight special days are known as the **Wheel of the Year**. The Wheel of the Year reflects the unending cycle of birth, life, harvest, death, and rebirth. Connecting with the Wheel of the Year and the rhythm of nature can enhance your magical work and bring balance to your life.

You can choose crystals to place outdoors on these dates to absorb the specific solar, lunar, and earthly energy of that event, and then carry those stones with you for a few days. Doing so will help you internalize these important changes in the seasons and how they're mirrored in your inner and outer life. The dates listed for some of the Sabbats are approximate; they can vary by a day or two from year to year. The exact dates for each year can be found on most calendars or in a farmers' almanac.

SAMHAIN, OCTOBER 31: This is a celebration of endings and rebirth. Samhain welcomes the dark months and honors the relationship between death and growth. It's also the night when many witches contact the spirits of their loved ones and venerate them. On this night, charge crystals outdoors that represent endings, banishing, and purification, such as black obsidian, calcite, and malachite.

YULE/WINTER SOLSTICE, DECEMBER 21: This marks the longest night of the year, and therefore the return of the sun. Yule is a time of strength, joy, and family. Lay out crystals that represent health, good cheer, and strength to carry you through the coldest, most fallow part of the year, such as green tourmaline, carnelian, and citrine.

IMBOLC, FEBRUARY 1: Imbolc is a celebration of light and fire. It marks the noticeably lengthening days and reminds us that warmer times are coming. Crystals appropriate for Imbolc represent hope, dreams, wishes, and goals for the coming months, including blue quartz, fire agate, and rainbow tourmaline.

OSTARA/SPRING EQUINOX, MARCH 21: This is the first day of spring, when flowers are pushing out of the ground and the earth is coming back to life. Crystals such as labradorite, agate, and lepidolite can be charged on this day for new beginnings, the birth of ideas and plans, and starting new ventures.

BELTANE/MAY DAY, MAY 1: This is a celebration of fertility and increase. Crystals you wish to charge with lust, productiveness, growth, romance, and union are aligned with this celebration. Some appropriate stones for Beltane are garnet, lodestone, and rhodochrosite.

LITHA/SUMMER SOLSTICE, JUNE 21: Litha marks the longest day of the year and focuses on solar powers such as vitality, production, and fruitfulness. Choose crystals that harness the abundance, fullness, and warmth of this day, such as sunstone, chrysanthemum stone, and topaz.

LAMMAS/LUGHNASADH, AUGUST 1: This is the first harvest celebration, when the grain is ready to be brought in. It's a time of thankfulness and reflection, as we think of all we've gained throughout the past months. Stones like unakite, brown jasper, and ruby charged during this time can help with the practice of gratitude and optimism.

MABON/AUTUMN EQUINOX, SEPTEMBER 21: Mabon marks the final harvest and the coming of the dark season. Day and night are of equal length on this day; after it, the nights become longer. It's a day for giving thanks, taking stock of what you have, and welcoming the transformation that comes with the winter. Stones charged at this time will have a feeling of completion, goals reached, and prosperity. Try pyrite, tigereye, and hag stones.

For those who don't celebrate the Wheel of the Year and prefer a more informal practice, there are other special days you can include in your crystal magic, such as your birthday, anniversaries, eclipses, meteor showers, and other celestial events.

Other Crystal Practices

The ways you can incorporate crystals into your witchcraft practice are limited only by your own creativity. Some witches carry so many crystals they're almost weighted down with stones, whereas others choose to work with just one at a time. Here are some of the diverse ways witches can integrate crystals into their craft.

LUNAR MAGIC: The full moon isn't the only time you can charge your crystals. The phases of the moon are an important element of a witch's life. The waxing moon is a time of increase and attraction magic, the full moon a time of illumination and intense power. The waning moon is for banishing, and the dark or new moon is for introspection and transformation. Crystals can be placed outdoors during these different phases to imbue them with the moon's influence. Consider making use of the new moon's energy for charging divination crystals, the waxing moon for prosperity or fertility crystals, the full moon for love and personal power, and the waning moon for removing unwanted energy.

DIVINATION: Some crystals are particularly aligned with psychic powers, such as amethyst, selenite, and moonstone. You can keep one or more of these crystals alongside your divination tools to amplify their accuracy and power.

ZODIAC SIGNS: Most people know about birthstones, and that each month is associated with a precious or semiprecious gem. The signs of the zodiac are also associated with specific crystals, and each sign isn't limited to just one. The crystals aligned with each zodiac sign are determined by the personality traits, strengths, and weaknesses of the sign, the planet ruling the sign, and which element the sign falls under. Carrying one of these crystals will increase the positive aspects of your sign while calming the less desirable traits. Find your zodiac sign below and choose one or more stones from the list. Carry them with you and see how they make you feel.

ARIES: Bloodstone, carnelian, and red jasper will complement your courage and high-spiritedness while grounding your quick temper.

TAURUS: Amber, malachite, and jade promote your stable and loyal side while helping you welcome new adventures so you don't get stuck.

GEMINI: Agate, labradorite, and opal complement your social, lovable traits while warding off indecision and flightiness.

CANCER: Moonstone, milky quartz, and selenite illuminate your deeply feeling, nurturing self while countering pessimism.

LEO: Onyx, iron pyrite, and sunstone highlight your generosity and courage while evening out your ego and pride.

VIRGO: Aventurine, amazonite, and peridot align with your brilliant intellect while quelling the desire to be controlling.

LIBRA: Amethyst, lapis lazuli, and tourmaline fit with your charisma and peaceful attitude while countering the need to constantly please everyone.

SCORPIO: Garnet, hematite, and rose quartz match your passion and determination while welcoming softer energy to calm vengeful and obsessive inclinations.

SAGITTARIUS: Aqua aura quartz, clear quartz, and aragonite complement your independent, philosophical nature while preventing tactlessness.

CAPRICORN: Jet, smoky quartz, and tigereye promote your ambition and resourcefulness while softening your stubborn edge.

AQUARIUS: Celestite, sodalite, and turquoise enhance your creativity and vision while keeping you in touch with your emotions.

PISCES: Aquamarine, fluorite, and pink kunzite help maintain your empathy and intuition while helping you overcome escapist behavior.

TAROT: Many tarot readers include crystals in their process. Crystals can cleanse, amplify, and empower your tarot deck. If your cards need to be purified after a difficult reading or an upset client, place some smoky quartz on top of the deck overnight to calm the intense energy. To increase psychic ability, charge some kyanite and keep it with your cards at all times. When doing a reading, place a clear quartz point nearby to clarify messages from the cards, making your readings more accurate.

OFFERINGS: Witches have a strong bond with our ancestors and loved ones who've passed into the spirit world. Taking the time to choose the right crystal for someone is an offering that shows respect and sends a message of love. You can place the crystal you choose at the gravesite or on your altar with a photograph of the person.

BROKEN CRYSTALS, LOST CRYSTALS

There may be nothing more distressing than discovering a favorite crystal companion you've been carrying with you for ages has broken. Or perhaps you can't find it anywhere. At worst it can feel like a bad omen, at best like you've lost something very important. When a crystal is lost or broken, it's a message—but not necessarily a negative one.

If you've recently discovered a broken crystal, there are many factors to consider when understanding its message. What were you feeling when it broke? Were you mid-conversation or ruminating about a problem you're having? A broken crystal is like a wake-up call: Pay attention to what's going on around you in the moment, because it's important to your life's path. Another reason a crystal may break is because its work with you is done and it's ready to go back into the earth. This can happen with stones that absorb so much energy that they rupture.

If your broken crystal is part of a spell, breakage can signify the release of the magic. Let it go and allow manifestation to happen. And remember, sometimes a broken crystal is just an ordinary accident. Don't panic. Respectfully bury it in the earth and move on.

If one of your trusty crystals gets a crack but remains intact, it's a signal to get ready for change. For example, if it's a love-drawing stone, it can mean someone special is on the way.

Losing a crystal is not any less painful, but the message behind is much more straightforward. It simply means that the stone is meant to go elsewhere right now. Someone who is meant to have it will find it. A lost crystal isn't, in fact, lost; it's on its way to exactly where it's supposed to be.

CRYSTAL COMPANIONS

30 Crystal Profiles

Agate 40

Amber 41

Amethyst 42

Aquamarine 43

Aventurine 44

Beryl 45

Calcite 46

Carnelian 47

Celestite 48

Chalcedony 49

Citrine 50

Fluorite 51

Garnet 52

Iron Pyrite 53

Jade 54

Jasper 55

Jet 56

Labradorite 57

Lapis Lazuli 58

Malachite 59

Moonstone 60

Obsidian 61

Onyx 62

Opal 63

Quartz 64

Selenite 65

Sunstone 66

Tigereye 67

Tourmaline 68

Turquoise 69

AGATE

There are many different types of agate, and all of them are associated with earth, grounding, and stabilizing. Agate can provide protection and balance while doing shadow work in your witchcraft practice. (For individual entries for black, blue lace, fire, and moss agate, see 100 Additional Crystals to Know on page 70.)

ORIGINS: Botswana, Brazil, India, Mexico, United States

COLORS: black, blue, brown, green, orange, pink, red, white

ASSOCIATED ENERGY CENTERS: Root Chakra

WORKS WELL WITH: ametrine, danburite

MAGICAL POWERS: Agate is very protective of children and babies. A stone of realism and pragmatism, agate helps you navigate difficult day-to-day situations in a way that builds character and results in growth.

PRACTICE SUGGESTIONS: Place agate in children's rooms to protect them from fear and nightmares. Agate encourages growth, so put some near your garden or specific plants or trees. Wear agate rings to be productive at your work or studies and prevent distraction.

TIP: Sew a tumbled agate into the hem of a child's jacket to create a protective shield around them.

AMBER

Amber is resin from evergreen trees that has hardened and fossilized. It can take millennia to form and sometimes has ancient plants or insects imbedded inside. Amber contains ancient tree energy, or the tree's "blood" in solid form.

ORIGINS: Baltic Sea, Canada, Italy, Poland, Russia, United States

COLORS: deep orange to light yellow

ASSOCIATED ENERGY CENTERS: Sacral Chakra, Solar Plexus Chakra

WORKS WELL WITH: jet, petrified wood, unakite

MAGICAL POWERS: Amber is an all-around amplifier of spells and is sacred to tree-loving witches. It's multipurpose, attracting protection, love, success, and money. Because of its age, it can help connect to ancestors.

PRACTICE SUGGESTIONS: Wearing a piece of amber intensifies a witch's magical power. Set aside a piece of amber jewelry that you wear only during spell casting and ritual. Doing so will increase its power and energy as well as your own.

TIP: Do not cleanse this resin with salt. Amber with insect or plant inclusions is worth more money, but it's equally magical with or without.

AMETHYST

Shimmering purple amethyst has been a well-known favorite for thousands of years. A highly spiritual stone, it can be found on many a witch's altar and magical jewelry.

ORIGINS: Argentina, Bolivia, Brazil, Canada, Madagascar, Mexico, United States, Zambia

COLORS: light to deep purple

ASSOCIATED ENERGY CENTERS: Crown Chakra, Third Eye Chakra

WORKS WELL WITH: ametrine, citrine, moonstone

MAGICAL POWERS: Amethyst is associated with pride and sobriety. It brings peace to the body, mind, and spirit. Amethyst is believed to create a clear connection to Spirit and the unseen world.

PRACTICE SUGGESTIONS: Amethyst can help break harmful habits. Empower one and carry it with you when trying to transform negative cycles in your own behavior. It will guide your spirit during this transition.

TIP: Amethyst heightens psychic ability. Keep some with your tarot cards or other divination tools. Darker amethyst may lose its color if left out in the sun.

AQUAMARINE

Light-blue aquamarine represents the sea and water goddesses. It was once carried by sailors to protect against drowning, negative spirits, and danger.

ORIGINS: Brazil, Kenya, Pakistan, United States, Zambia

COLORS: greenish blue

ASSOCIATED ENERGY CENTERS: Throat Chakra

WORKS WELL WITH: mica, moonstone, sunstone

MAGICAL POWERS: Aquamarine can be rubbed on the body to cleanse and purify your energetic field. It brings peace to the body and mind and can be included in spells for emotional clarity.

PRACTICE SUGGESTIONS: Wear aquamarine for protection when traveling over bodies of water by plane or boat. Create an elixir by placing aquamarine in water, and drink it to cleanse your aura. Don't forget to remove the crystal before drinking.

TIP: Aquamarine can fade when exposed to too much light, so avoid charging or cleansing it in direct sun.

AVENTURINE

Aventurine crystals contain speckles of other minerals, which create a mystical sparkling affect. It's a stone of deep perception and imagination that leads to new life paths. Aventurine can ease emotional pain and heal a broken heart.

ORIGINS: Austria, Brazil, China, India, Russia, Tanzania

COLORS: light blue, light green, peach

ASSOCIATED ENERGY CENTERS: Heart Chakra

WORKS WELL WITH: snowflake obsidian, tiger iron

MAGICAL POWERS: Aventurine enhances workings that are meant to increase mental capacity, intellect, and discernment. It can help locate and harness opportunities when you feel stuck. Green aventurine is included in spells for money, prosperity, and material gain.

PRACTICE SUGGESTIONS: When dealing with a broken heart, wear aventurine on a necklace near your heart to help you heal. It will open your mind to new opportunities that allow you to move forward.

TIP: Some people tape aventurine to their cell phone to protect against its emanations.

BERYL

Beryl is a calming stone that is also good for scrying and divination. It's carried to increase courage, reduce stress, and in ancient times was believed to bring rain.

ORIGINS: Australia, Brazil, Russia, United States

COLORS: blue, gold, pink

ASSOCIATED ENERGY CENTERS: Crown Chakra, Solar Plexus Chakra

WORKS WELL WITH: serpentine, tourmaline

MAGICAL POWERS: Beryl can guard against the manipulation and ill intention of others and is included in spells to halt gossip. It's also believed to enhance intelligence and wisdom while quieting fear.

PRACTICE SUGGESTIONS: Carry a piece of beryl when you're struggling to make a difficult decision. It opens intuitive channels and allows messages to come through from Spirit to mind. Keep a piece of beryl near the bathtub or shower for purification.

TIP: Beryl is connected to sea gods and goddesses and can be placed on your altar to represent them.

CALCITE

Calcite comes in a range of colors that can be applied to clearing, purifying, and stabilizing different areas of life. Calcite enhances mystical experiences such as meditation, prayer, and contacting spirits.

ORIGINS: Brazil, Britain, Iceland, United States

COLORS: blue, clear, green, orange, pink

ASSOCIATED ENERGY CENTERS: All chakras, especially Crown Chakra

WORKS WELL WITH: all stones

MAGICAL POWERS: Calcite lets you send energy to others from a distance. Pink calcite brings love, blue aids healing, green attracts prosperity, and clear calcite purifies people and objects.

PRACTICE SUGGESTIONS: Place a calcite crystal on the third eye (on the forehead) when meditating and it will strengthen your ability to control and direct energy in your magic.

TIP: If you see a rainbow in a piece of clear calcite, it means new beginnings and a fresh start are on their way to you. Do not immerse in water or salt.

CARNELIAN

Carnelian is an orange stone associated with success, power, and vitality. It's connected to the element of fire and the sun, making it a repository of passion and determination.

ORIGINS: Brazil, India, United States, Uruguay

COLORS: orange, red

ASSOCIATED ENERGY CENTERS: Sacral Chakra

WORKS WELL WITH: aquamarine, beryl, super seven

MAGICAL POWERS: Carnelian is included in spells for success, confidence, and motivation. It can bring about a burst of inspiration and energy and is sometimes used in sex magic.

PRACTICE SUGGESTIONS: Place carnelian in your work area to boost productivity. To break through lethargy and boredom, meditate with it placed on your sacral area, just below your navel. Carry it with you to make a good impression on others.

TIP: Let your carnelian bask in direct sun regularly to keep its energy powerful.

CELESTITE

Celestite creates understanding of the universe and the interconnectedness of all living things. It enhances astral travel and dream states and encourages spiritual enlightenment. It develops confidence in your own magical abilities.

ORIGINS: Britain, Egypt, Madagascar, Mexico

COLORS: blue, white, yellow

ASSOCIATED ENERGY CENTERS: Crown Chakra, Third Eye Chakra, Throat Chakra

WORKS WELL WITH: blue lace agate, moldavite, selenite

MAGICAL POWERS: Celestite helps produce prophetic dreams. It creates harmony during disagreements by cooling the emotions, and it opens the mind to higher vibrations, which helps invoke Spirit in rituals and spells.

PRACTICE SUGGESTIONS: Place celestite in a room where an argument has taken place to cleanse and restore it to peace. Keep a piece on your altar to represent Spirit or deity.

TIP: Celestite will fade when exposed to too much sunlight and will be damaged by water.

CHALCEDONY

Chalcedony is a nurturing, loving stone inspiring benevolence, generosity, and care. It's associated with bonding between mother and child and is said to increase lactation. It's a crystal for healers and empaths.

ORIGINS: Austria, Brazil, Britain, Mexico, Morocco, United States

COLORS: blue, gray, pink, white

ASSOCIATED ENERGY CENTERS: Crown Chakra, Sacral Chakra

WORKS WELL WITH: aragonite, flint

MAGICAL POWERS: Chalcedony prevents fear and wards off nightmares, psychic attacks, and curses. It's believed to dispel unhealthy illusions and to offer protection against intrusive thoughts and feelings that come from others.

PRACTICE SUGGESTIONS: Keep a piece of chalcedony near your bed to prevent disturbing dreams. Carry it with you to overcome anger and hostility, or give a piece to someone who needs it.

TIP: White chalcedony surrounds you with calm, caring energy when dealing with distressed or troubled people.

CITRINE

Cheerful yellow citrine encapsulates the power of the sun: joy, warmth, abundance, and connection. It energizes everything around it and strengthens your ability to manifest your goals.

ORIGINS: Brazil, Madagascar, Russia, United States

COLORS: brown, translucent yellow

ASSOCIATED ENERGY CENTERS: Solar Plexus Chakra

WORKS WELL WITH: amethyst, ametrine, topaz

MAGICAL POWERS: Citrine is a powerful manifestation stone and can be added to grids and spells for this purpose. It's associated with prosperity, success in business, and career opportunities. Carry it to inspire creative new ideas.

PRACTICE SUGGESTIONS: Place citrine in a room where positive communication is needed, such as a boardroom or family room. Citrine also incites courage when facing change and new situations, especially in the workplace.

TIP: Amethyst is often heat treated to make it turn yellow and sold as citrine. Natural citrine is a consistent honey color, whereas fake citrine is white on the bottom and dark yellow at the top. Citrine can lose its color if it's left in direct sunlight.

FLUORITE

Fluorite aligns the mind, body, and spirit to create a sense of balance and wholeness. It's believed to provide mental focus and stimulate the intellect. (For individual entries for blue, clear, green, purple, rainbow, and yellow fluorite, see 100 Additional Crystals to Know on page 70.)

ORIGINS: Brazil, Britain, Canada, China, Germany, United States

COLORS: blue, clear, green, purple

ASSOCIATED ENERGY CENTERS: Third Eye Chakra, Throat Chakra

WORKS WELL WITH: kyanite, labradorite, lapis lazuli

MAGICAL POWERS: Fluorite can bring structure to a chaotic life and control overwhelming emotions. It helps you retain information and is excellent for spells related to studying, tests, and examinations. Keep some fluorite with your witchcraft books to help you learn.

PRACTICE SUGGESTIONS: Place fluorite in your palm to quell stress and worries that are in the way of productivity. Wear fluorite jewelry when you need to be objective and intelligent.

TIP: Fluorite is protective against the harmful electromagnetic fields emitted by various technologies. Keep some with your cell phone or computer. Fluorite may fade in direct sunlight.

GARNET

Bloodred garnet is a stone of health, sensuality, and strength. It symbolizes the heart, desire, love, passion, and sexuality. Garnet is also a protection stone that shields the aura completely.

ORIGINS: Worldwide

COLORS: dark red

ASSOCIATED ENERGY CENTERS: Heart Chakra, Root Chakra

WORKS WELL WITH: emerald, howlite, ruby, snow quartz

MAGICAL POWERS: Garnet is popular for love and attraction spells. It can ensure commitment in relationships or guide you to a suitable partner with whom you have both physical and mental chemistry.

PRACTICE SUGGESTIONS: Wear a garnet close to your heart when trying to decide between two relationships. It will lead you to the person who is best for you long term.

TIP: Wear a garnet to prolong your energy when you're exercising or studying hard.

IRON PYRITE

Iron pyrite is sometimes called fool's gold because it looks so similar to real gold that it's often mistaken for it. Pyrite symbolizes money, prosperity, riches, and material things.

ORIGINS: Britain, Canada, Italy, United States

COLORS: shiny gold

ASSOCIATED ENERGY CENTERS: Solar Plexus Chakra

WORKS WELL WITH: hematite, quartz, tigereye

MAGICAL POWERS: Iron pyrite is used in all kinds of money attraction spells, for success in business, and luck in gambling. Pyrite can create an aura of authority and confidence and boost your creativity.

PRACTICE SUGGESTIONS: Tie a piece of pyrite, some peppermint, and a coin together in a small bit of green cloth to make a lucky prosperity charm.

TIP: Pyrite naturally grows in sturdy cubes that make it even more effective for promoting financial stability. Don't place iron pyrite in water.

JADE

Jade is sacred throughout the Far East and has become known around the world as a stone of prosperity, longevity, wisdom, and luck. It also attracts goodwill and friendship.

ORIGINS: China, Middle East, Russia, United States

COLORS: all shades of green, orange, purple, red, yellow

ASSOCIATED ENERGY CENTERS: Heart Chakra

WORKS WELL WITH: larimar, prehnite

MAGICAL POWERS: Jade is given as a gift to signify love. When worn over the heart, it can open you to affection and sensitivity. Amulets, animal figures, and coins are made of jade to attract business success, money, and health.

PRACTICE SUGGESTIONS: Wear jade jewelry on your left finger or arm to attract prosperous energy. Wear it on your right arm or finger to bestow generosity on others.

TIP: The deeper its shade of green, the more valuable the jade is. Dark green translucent pieces known as imperial jade are the most coveted.

JASPER

Jasper is a stone of health and protection. It is available in many colors, each with its own unique vibration. Jasper is very solid and has a protective, stabilizing feel to it, bringing a sense of wholeness and safety. (For individual entries for blue, brown, green, mookaite, picture, red, and yellow jasper, see 100 Additional Crystals to Know on page 70.)

ORIGINS: Worldwide

COLORS: black, blue, brown, green, patterned, red, yellow

ASSOCIATED ENERGY CENTERS: Root Chakra

WORKS WELL WITH: celestite, diamond, petrified wood

MAGICAL POWERS: Jasper can be added to spells for healing, protection, confidence, and stability. Its range of colors makes it very versatile, bringing strength and solidity to all kinds of spells.

PRACTICE SUGGESTIONS: Jasper can act as an anchor for your thoughts and feelings, helping you keep them grounded in reality. Carry one with you while trying to be assertive and confident.

TIP: Arrowheads carved from jasper are carried as good luck charms.

JET

Jet is wood that has fossilized over millions of years into a hard black mass. It's believed that it absorbs part of the soul of anyone it touches. Jet is sometimes called witch's amber.

ORIGINS: United States

COLORS: black

ASSOCIATED ENERGY CENTERS: Crown Chakra, Root Chakra

WORKS WELL WITH: amber, clear quartz, petrified wood

MAGICAL POWERS: Jet is a powerfully protective stone that can siphon bad vibes out of a situation or person. This quality makes it useful in banishing and binding rituals.

PRACTICE SUGGESTIONS: To remove negativity from a person, place jet over their heart while visualizing it pulling out the problem. Wrap the stone completely in black cotton ribbon and bury it in the earth.

TIP: Sometimes black glass is sold as French jet, but it isn't authentic. Real jet is very light and warm to the touch, whereas the imitation is cold and heavy.

LABRADORITE

Labradorite is a dark stone with iridescent colors that change in the light shimmering on its surface. It's a stone of mysticism, occult, and magic, sacred to seers and witches.

ORIGINS: Australia, Canada, Finland, Madagascar

COLORS: iridescent black or gray

ASSOCIATED ENERGY CENTERS: Third Eye Chakra

WORKS WELL WITH: jet, opal, peacock ore

MAGICAL POWERS: Labradorite is dark, with all the colors within it, much like dark earth contains everything needed for growth. This stone can bring your mystical qualities to the surface and enhance your natural magical abilities.

PRACTICE SUGGESTIONS: Labradorite is the ultimate witch's stone. Keep some on your altar to signify the power of witchcraft and strengthen your altar's energetic imprint. Wear it as jewelry to help you see the magic of everyday life while learning your craft.

TIP: Labradorite can dissolve in water, so it's best to cleanse it with moonlight, smoke, or sunlight.

LAPIS LAZULI

Lapis lazuli is a dark blue stone with sparkling pyrite scattered throughout it like stars. It's a stone of spiritual awareness and can help in understanding the path of the soul.

ORIGINS: Afghanistan, Middle East, United States

COLORS: blue

ASSOCIATED ENERGY CENTERS: Third Eye Chakra, Throat Chakra

WORKS WELL WITH: phantom quartz, purple tourmaline

MAGICAL POWERS: Lapis lazuli increases psychic ability and connection to the spirit world. It's used to reverse baneful magic and increase personal power.

PRACTICE SUGGESTIONS: Wearing earrings made of lapis lazuli will open you to receiving messages from Spirit as you navigate your magical path. It will help you be authentic to yourself and others.

TIP: This stone is soft and porous, making it crack and chip easily. Keep it away from water and salt.

MALACHITE

Malachite has mesmerizing patterns of deep, rich green. It's an intense stone that brings about drastic changes, new beginnings, and dramatic transformation.

ORIGINS: Russia, Zaire

COLORS: bands and rings of green

ASSOCIATED ENERGY CENTERS: Heart Chakra

WORKS WELL WITH: black obsidian, rose quartz, spinel

MAGICAL POWERS: Malachite is used in spells that bring huge, life-altering changes. It can present risks that will help you grow, break unhealthy ties, create necessary endings, and destroy things that stand in your way.

PRACTICE SUGGESTIONS: If your malachite breaks into pieces, it can be a warning that negativity is coming and you need to protect your energy.

TIP: Malachite is toxic, so don't use it in elixirs. It's also damaged when exposed to water and salt.

MOONSTONE

Moonstone is a favorite among witches for its lunar power and connection to moon goddesses. Many witches integrate this crystal into their practice in tandem with the moon phases.

ORIGINS: Australia, Brazil, India, Sri Lanka

COLORS: cream, gray, iridescent, milky white, pink

ASSOCIATED ENERGY CENTERS: Crown Chakra, Sacral Chakra, Solar Plexus Chakra

WORKS WELL WITH: aquamarine, garnet, pearl

MAGICAL POWERS: Moonstone is used in spells to attract lasting emotional love and resolve misunderstandings in relationships. It increases psychic powers and enhances your affinity with the rhythm of the lunar cycles. It's a stone of sensuality.

PRACTICE SUGGESTIONS: Place a moonstone on your solar plexus during meditation to help heal emotional wounds. Pregnant people should carry moonstone.

TIP: Don't cleanse moonstone with salt. Opalite, a type of glass, is often sold as "rainbow moonstone," named for its colorful shimmer. It doesn't have the magical powers of moonstone.

OBSIDIAN

Obsidian is black volcanic glass, formed when molten lava hits cold water or air and solidifies. It's an example of how destruction and creation are clearly linked and holds the power of both fire and ice.

ORIGINS: Anywhere there is volcanic activity

COLORS: black, blue, brown, green

ASSOCIATED ENERGY CENTERS: Root Chakra

WORKS WELL WITH: howlite, malachite

MAGICAL POWERS: Obsidian spheres or polished pieces are used for scrying and divination. Obsidian is very protective and no-nonsense; when you carry it, you will see the clear truth about what needs to change in your life.

PRACTICE SUGGESTIONS: Wear an obsidian arrowhead to detect and overcome challenges. Obsidian is an excellent material for an athame.

TIP: In ancient times weapons were fashioned from obsidian, which make them powerful in protection spells.

ONYX

It was once believed that onyx held a demon or evil force inside of it that could destroy relationships. Some people consider it a protective stone instead. Try meditating with onyx to see how it resonates with you.

ORIGINS: Brazil, India, South Africa, United States

COLORS: black

ASSOCIATED ENERGY CENTERS: Root Chakra

WORKS WELL WITH: diamond, rhodonite

MAGICAL POWERS: Onyx boosts personal power when facing adversaries or difficult situations. It can be included in spells for protection from danger and to reverse curses.

PRACTICE SUGGESTIONS: Stash a piece of black onyx in your pocket or bag when you know you're entering a situation where people bear you ill will, whatever the reason. It will protect you from their thoughts.

TIP: Onyx is believed to hold on to all the memories of the person who carries it. If you're keeping secrets, don't let anyone get their hands on your onyx!

OPAL

Opal contains many different powers within it because of its colorful shimmer, which is called opalescence. Opal absorbs energy and then sends it back to its source.

ORIGINS: Australia, Brazil, Canada, Mexico, United States

COLORS: black, brown, green, purple, red, white, yellow

ASSOCIATED ENERGY CENTERS: Heart Chakra, Solar Plexus Chakra

WORKS WELL WITH: labradorite, red tourmaline

MAGICAL POWERS: Opal can bring inner beauty to the surface and helps recall past lives. Black opal is worn during spell casting to increase the magical power of the witch.

PRACTICE SUGGESTIONS: Empower an opal with invisibility and carry it with you. You won't physically disappear, but you will go unnoticed by others.

TIP: Opal will be damaged by salt and can fade in direct sunlight, so cleanse it with other crystals, smoke, or moonlight.

QUARTZ

Quartz is one of the best-known and bountiful minerals in the earth. Although common, it possesses great power, directs energy, and amplifies any intention. (For individual entries for aqua aura, blue, golden, green, lithium, phantom, rose, smoky, and spirit quartz, see 100 Additional Crystals to Know on page 70.)

ORIGINS: Worldwide

COLORS: blue, clear, gray, green, orange, pink, purple

ASSOCIATED ENERGY CENTERS: Crown Chakra

WORKS WELL WITH: All other crystals

MAGICAL POWERS: Clear quartz can be empowered with almost any intention. It automatically aligns energetically with the person it touches, making it a perfect fit for any personal need. It clears away stagnant energy.

PRACTICE SUGGESTIONS: Place a quartz tower on your altar to strengthen every ritual done there. Aim a quartz point at an object you wish to imbue with extra power.

TIP: Quartz amplifies any stones it's placed with, making it excellent in grids and for general practice. Quartz can act as a substitute for any other crystal.

SELENITE

Selenite is ghostly white and possesses a luminous spiritual energy. Its name comes from Selene, an ancient Greek moon goddess.

ORIGINS: Austria, Britain, France, Mexico, Russia, United States

COLORS: brown, green, sometimes orange, white

ASSOCIATED ENERGY CENTERS: Crown Chakra

WORKS WELL WITH: black tourmaline, brown jasper, kyanite

MAGICAL POWERS: Selenite accesses Spirit and the higher consciousness, making it an ideal stone for meditation. It can also clear negativity from your aura. Selenite is known for both cleansing and charging all other crystals.

PRACTICE SUGGESTIONS: Hold a selenite wand in your hand and move it over your entire body from head to toe several times. Allow it to draw out all disruptive or unwanted vibrations.

TIP: Selenite reacts badly to salt and water. It can be delicate and should be stored carefully.

SUNSTONE

Sunstone contains the power of the sun, positivity, warmth, growth, and fame. It attracts positive attention and a winning attitude.

ORIGINS: Canada, India, Norway, United States

COLORS: brown, orange, yellow

ASSOCIATED ENERGY CENTERS: Sacral Chakra, Solar Plexus Chakra

WORKS WELL WITH: citrine, mica, yellow jasper

MAGICAL POWERS: Sunstone creates an inner fire that vanquishes any unwanted power others hold over you, helping you break free so you can fearlessly shine as your authentic self. It's a stone of self-love and confidence.

PRACTICE SUGGESTIONS: Place a sunstone over a picture of a person who is trying to hold you back. Its fiery brightness will blot out their influence like a blinding sun ray, allowing you to step into your power.

TIP: Sunstone sometimes contains shimmering particles of hematite, which is a natural magnet, making it especially good for attraction magic.

TIGEREYE

Tigereye contains both earth and sun energy, making it versatile for many magical workings. It unites ideas with matter, helping manifest your goals.

ORIGINS: Mexico, South Africa, United States

COLORS: blue, brown and gold, red

ASSOCIATED ENERGY CENTERS: Solar Plexus Chakra, Third Eye Chakra

WORKS WELL WITH: cat's-eye, chalcedony, topaz

MAGICAL POWERS: Tigereye is a stone for integrity, pride, and justice. Its authoritative vibration can be overwhelming to some, in which case it can be placed alongside a complementary stone to soften its effect.

PRACTICE SUGGESTIONS: Empower a tigereye to seek the truth and carry it with you when you wish to detect a liar. They will be outed one way or another. Include tigereye in spells related to the legal system.

TIP: Wear tigereye near your solar plexus to increase confidence and near your throat to help you speak the truth.

TOURMALINE

Tourmaline is excellent at divining the correct course of action, providing protection during rituals, and helping understand one's deepest inner self. (For individual entries for black, blue, brown, green, pink, purple, rainbow, red, and watermelon tourmaline, see 100 Additional Crystals to Know on page 70.)

ORIGINS: Brazil, Madagascar, Namibia, Nigeria, Sri Lanka, Tanzania, United States

COLORS: black, blue, brown, pink, purple, red, yellow

ASSOCIATED ENERGY CENTERS: Root Chakra, Throat Chakra

WORKS WELL WITH: lepidolite, mica, selenite

MAGICAL POWERS: Tourmaline protects sensitive and empathic people from being drained by the emotions of others. It creates a shield between your own aura and incoming energy, allowing peace to flourish.

PRACTICE SUGGESTIONS: To ensure peaceful sleep, place black tourmaline in the window of a room you'd like to protect from outside negativity. Wear tourmaline jewelry for spiritual protection.

TIP: Tourmaline comes in many colors. Try meditating with different shades to figure out just how each works for you. Keep them away from water.

TURQUOISE

Turquoise is considered a master stone of healing, positivity, prosperity, and life-giving energy. It's been revered by people for thousands of years as a healer and protector.

ORIGINS: Afghanistan, China, Iran, Mexico, United States

COLORS: blue, green, turquoise

ASSOCIATED ENERGY CENTERS: Throat Chakra, Third Eye Chakra

WORKS WELL WITH: marble, sunstone

MAGICAL POWERS: Turquoise is believed to absorb the vibrations of whoever touches it, cleansing them of unwanted energy. It's said that the stone will fade or break when overloaded. Turquoise is associated with environmental awareness and can strengthen your connection to the earth and elements.

PRACTICE SUGGESTIONS: Wear turquoise rings to enhance your powers when performing healing rituals. Place turquoise over any part of the body that feels pain or unease to help draw it out.

TIP: Sometimes howlite stones are dyed and sold as turquoise. Real turquoise is often also dyed to brighten its color, although this doesn't affect its magical power. Don't immerse turquoise in water or salt, and keep it out of direct sunlight.

100 Additional Crystals to Know

Agate: Black 72

Agate: Blue Lace 72

Agate: Fire 72

Agate: Moss 72

Alexandrite 72

Amazonite 72

Ametrine 72

Ammolite Shell 73

Angelite 73

Apache Tears 73

Apatite 73

Aragonite 73

Azurite 73

Bloodstone 74

Boji Stones 74

Bronzite 74

Cat's-Eye 74

Chrysanthemum Stone 74

Chrysocolla 74

Chrysoprase 75

Coral 75

Dalmatian Stone 75

Danburite 75

Diamond 75

Desert Rose 75

Dioptase 76

Emerald 76

Epidote 76

Flint 76

Fluorite: Blue 76

Fluorite: Clear 76

Fluorite: Green 76

Fluorite: Purple 77

Fluorite: Rainbow 77

Fluorite: Yellow 77

Fuchsite 77

Girasol 77

Hag Stone 77

Howlite 78

Iceland Spar 78

Iolite 78

Jasper: Blue 78

Jasper: Brown 78

Jasper: Green 78

Jasper: Mookaite 79

Jasper: Picture 79

Jasper: Red 79

Jasper: Yellow 79

Kunzite 79

Kyanite 79

Larimar 80

Lava Rock 80

Lepidolite 80

Lodestone/Magnetite 80

Marble 80

Merlinite 80

Meteorite 80

Mica 81

Moldavite 81

Mother of Pearl 81

Peacock Ore 81

Pearl 81

Peridot 81

Petrified Wood 82

Prehnite 82

Pumice 82

Purpurite 82

Quartz: Aqua Aura 82

Quartz: Blue 82

Quartz: Golden 83

Quartz: Green 83

Quartz: Lithium 83

Quartz: Phantom 83

Quartz: Rose 83

Quartz: Smoky 83

Quartz: Spirit 83

Rhodochrosite 84

Rhodonite 84

Ruby 84

Sapphire 84

Sardonyx 84

Serpentine 84

Snowflake Obsidian 85

Sodalite 85

Spinel 85

Sugilite 85

Super Seven 85

Tiger Iron 85

Topaz 85

Tourmaline: Black 86

Tourmaline: Blue 86

Tourmaline: Brown 86

Tourmaline: Green 86

Tourmaline: Pink 86

Tourmaline: Purple 86

Tourmaline: Rainbow 87

Tourmaline: Red 87

Tourmaline: Watermelon 87

Unakite 87

Zircon 87

Agate: Black

Black agate is solid and protective. It guards material objects such as the home and its contents. Place some near your valuables or where you keep your jewelry. It's also carried to win competitions.

Agate: Blue Lace

Gentle and calming, blue lace agate can be included in workings for kindness, self-acceptance, and healing from judgment and shame. It helps people talk about their feelings and reduces anger.

Agate: Fire

Fire agate reverses the ill intent of others, sending it back to the source while also protecting you. It can give direction to your inner passions and dreams.

Agate: Moss

Moss agate promotes growth of all kinds, including your own garden and houseplants. It helps uncover treasure and attracts prosperity in unexpected ways.

Alexandrite

It's said that alexandrite contains all the esoteric information once kept in the ancient library of Alexandria. Its two-tone shimmer can help you see things from new perspectives.

Amazonite

Amazonite enables you to speak your truth and stand up for yourself. It encourages creativity and helps you proudly share your ideas. It can facilitate communication in an emotionally blocked person.

Ametrine

Keep ametrine nearby while astral traveling to defend against psychic attack or negative energy that's sent toward you. Ametrine can anchor peace inside of you so that you're unaffected by surrounding chaos.

Ammolite Shell

The spiral shape of ammolite symbolizes the never-ending cycles of nature, life, and the cosmos and helps you understand your place within it all. Ammolite helps you accept the impermanence of earthly life.

Angelite

Keep angelite near when learning about the stars, astrology, and planetary influences. It creates a telepathic link between people; give a piece to someone so you can share mental messages with each other from afar.

Apache Tears

Apache tears are small pieces of tumbled black obsidian, a form of volcanic glass. These stones are carried to help work through grief and loss, particularly the death of a loved one.

Apatite

Apatite promotes kindness, humanitarianism, generosity, and universal love. It's an excellent stone for spells that encourage harmonious teamwork for the greater good. Apatite resonates with volunteers and selfless people who donate their time to important causes.

Aragonite

Aragonite helps release past hardships to welcome new growth in life and amplify bravery. It's effective for attuning with the earth element and creates mindfulness of the environment. Do not immerse it in water.

Azurite

Azurite breaks old patterns of thought. When your upbringing or conditioning is holding you back, azurite can help you recognize these blockages and grow beyond them. It also increases psychic ability. Do not immerse it in water or salt.

Bloodstone

In ancient Egypt, bloodstone was believed to open doors and remove walls. Bloodstone can be added to spells for overcoming obstacles or unearthing secrets. It brings victory in court cases. Because of its green color, it's associated with prosperity.

Boji Stones

Boji stones are earthy brown rocks that bring grounding and stability. You need a male and female stone; female stones are rounded and male stones are angled. Hold them together in your hand to simultaneously energize and balance yourself.

Bronzite

Bronzite helps you be in the now, making it a great aid for people who struggle with being still and achieving meditative states due to racing thoughts. Bronzite will harness a curse and amplify it back onto the sender.

Cat's-Eye

Cat's-eye can be placed near your beauty products because it's believed to increase attractiveness. It enhances inner vision and perception; you can empower a cat's-eye to find out specific information or see that which is hidden.

Chrysanthemum Stone

This stone brings luck and harmony, helping you function at your absolute best. It heightens mystical experiences, helping you see deeper meaning in the everyday and giving you spiritual support at all times. Chrysanthemum stone can help you bloom into your full potential as a witch.

Chrysocolla

Chrysocolla is a stone of discretion, so keep one near that which you want to keep secret. It's also associated with wisdom and can guide you about when to hold your tongue and when to speak out.

Chrysoprase

Perfect for artists, chrysoprase increases creativity and talent. It also encourages fidelity, forgiveness, compassion, and nonjudgmental thinking in relationships, while banishing greed and selfishness.

Coral

Finding a piece of coral will grant you the powers of the ocean: plumbing deep emotion, comprehending hidden undercurrents, and accessing wisdom usually hidden from human eyes. Source coral very carefully and responsibly, because it comes from a living being. Only keep bits that you find naturally and that are already dead. These are gifts from the sea and are very special.

Dalmatian Stone

Dalmatian stone is said to send an energetic warning when danger is near, so pay attention to the vibration it's giving out. It can calm obsessive thoughts and help you forget your worries. It also encourages a sense of playfulness and a carefree attitude.

Danburite

Place danburite in a room to drain the stress and strain out of it. Danburite brings love and comfort to people who need it during grief, loss, breakups, or life's general clamor.

Diamond

Diamonds represent self-confidence, sensuality, and sexual openness. A status symbol, any size diamond can be empowered to attract attention and admiration. They're also used in prosperity spells.

Desert Rose

Desert rose encompasses the witch's motto, "As above, so below," because it contains both selenite (associated with the moon) and sand (the earth). It bonds the element of Spirit with the element of earth, creating a beautiful synchronicity between the physical and astral realms—just as you do when you cast a spell.

Dioptase

Dioptase heals betrayal and sorrow, helping you overcome anger and bitterness. It helps identify and release people or situations that are holding you back or entities that have attached to you.

Emerald

Emerald brings knowledge of the past, present, and future. It stimulates cooperation, increasing domestic peace and loyalty in a partnership. If your emerald changes color, it signifies infidelity in love.

Epidote

Epidote stirs up pain and resentment you're holding on to so it can be released. It helps avert the mindset of victimhood and prevents gullibility. Only use this stone when you're truly ready to face your own dark side.

Flint

Knives, weapons, and protection amulets made of flint have been found worldwide. Place a piece of flint above your front door to defend your home and family, or carry a piece with you to avert danger.

Fluorite: Blue

Blue fluorite organizes thoughts and allows clear communication. It can help you gather your scattered feelings into effectively explained ideas in a debate or disagreement.

Fluorite: Clear

Clear fluorite can help Spirit manifest in your life in a way that your rational mind plainly understands. This quality makes it a great crystal for the beginner witch who's trying to grasp new magical concepts.

Fluorite: Green

Green fluorite is for entrepreneurs. Associated with prosperity and mental clarity, it can aid in figuring out business strategies and finding creative ways to make your projects succeed. Another green stone that symbolizes growth and increase, it can help get an undertaking off the ground.

Fluorite: Purple

Purple fluorite strengthens psychic ability and is another stone best kept with your oracle of choice. It helps your conscious mind interpret divination symbols and apply them to everyday life. It clarifies communication between yourself and a querent (one who seeks an answer), if you read for others.

Fluorite: Rainbow

Rainbow fluorite is a combination of blue, green, clear, and purple and therefore possesses a little bit of each of their individual energies. This makes it a very powerful, sought-after stone.

Fluorite: Yellow

Yellow fluorite stimulates the intellect and facilitates group activities and teamwork. It helps everyone involved work together with heightened understanding of one another and the shared task.

Fuchsite

Fuchsite is an excellent helper for witches who work with herbs. Keep some nearby when mixing up your own herbal remedies to boost their efficacy and increase your magical connection to the plants. Do not immerse it in water.

Girasol

Girasol assists with difficult transformations, helping you ease through big changes like moving, divorce, and switching jobs. It helps you stay focused, preventing feelings of being emotionally overwhelmed.

Hag Stone

A hag stone is any rock with a hole naturally worn through it, usually by water. Finding a hag stone is incredibly lucky. String it on a cord and wear it for everything from prosperity to protection.

Howlite

Howlite uncovers past lives and can help you access other dimensions and times. It can be included in spells for peace, as it slows an overactive mind, especially when you're trying to sleep. It has a very soft, soothing energy.

Iceland Spar

Iceland spar can reveal hidden information or help you understand the secret meaning behind words and symbols. It allows you to read between the lines in conversation and understand what's *not* being said. Do not immerse it in water.

Iolite

Iolite is believed to help in overcoming addictions and bad habits of all kinds. It aids in self-expression, discovering your own inner strength, and realizing your own value, which are all beneficial when restarting your life.

Jasper: Blue

Blue jasper reveals the bit of positivity present in all situations, no matter how small. It can open your mind to the bigger picture so you understand the purpose of life's challenges.

Jasper: Brown

Brown jasper strengthens your connection to the earth. If you have to spend your time indoors, disconnected from nature, try carrying a bit of brown jasper to keep some condensed earth energy nearby.

Jasper: Green

Green jasper makes a great amulet to attract physical health and stamina. It balances aspects of life that have become unmanageable, such as obsessions, toxic relationships, and damaging thought and behavior patterns.

Jasper: Mookaite

Mookaite can help you make important decisions about your future. It gives you fresh ideas for how to proceed in situations that have become stagnant by bringing new perspectives to your attention.

Jasper: Picture

Picture jasper has clear, dark lines that will speak directly to you at first glance. Take note of what shapes and symbols are in the markings and consider what they mean when applied to your own life.

Jasper: Red

Red jasper is a solid, stabilizing stone that brings balance, practicality, and sound judgment. It will help you keep your feet on the ground while bringing slow, steady beneficial change.

Jasper: Yellow

Yellow jasper increases self-confidence and the ability to deal with problems in practical and mature ways. It deflects overly emotional reactions and instills you with capability and calm.

Kunzite

Kunzite brings calm and peace to stressful environments. It encourages humility and helps you analyze your own behavior and mistakes. It can also banish unwanted negative energy that has attached itself to you. Kunzite can fade with prolonged exposure to sunlight.

Kyanite

Kyanite creates clear, prophetic dreams and helps you remember them. Keep a piece with your dream journal for this purpose. Kyanite carries ideas from Spirit to your mind, so you can then manifest them in reality.

Larimar

Larimar attracts the right people into your life at the right time. It can help you find a soul mate and identify those who will guide you to your true purpose in life.

Lava Rock

Porous volcanic rock can absorb energy and store it until you need it. It can also siphon unwanted energy out of a room or situation. Be sure to cleanse it afterward.

Lepidolite

Lepidolite brings peace and calm to place or person. It cleans up energetic mess and organizes it into productive channels. It can disrupt old modes of thinking, allowing growth to begin.

Lodestone/Magnetite

Lodestone is a naturally occurring magnet, carrying both a negative and a positive charge. It can be used in spells for both attraction and banishing. Because it can do two opposing things, a clear intention is very important.

Marble

Marble is protective and grounding, making it an excellent stone for an altar top. It helps you become master of your own thoughts and intentions.

Merlinite

Merlinite attracts magical, mystical energy of all kinds because it contains the collective power of magicians, alchemists, shamans, witches, and all magical people. It carries your thoughts to Spirit to manifest.

Meteorite

A meteorite contains great knowledge from beyond the earth realm. Treasure your meteorite and it will grant you knowledge about life's biggest questions, such as life after death and the purpose of existence itself.

Mica

Mica helps you focus on the present. It allows you to let go of things you cannot control outside of yourself, bringing peace and acceptance of your current situation. Keep some with you when practicing mindfulness.

Moldavite

Moldavite formed when a meteor struck the earth. It contains celestial vibrations, unlike earthly crystals. Moldavite reveals the magic at work in your everyday life in the form of synchronicities and meaningful symbols.

Mother of Pearl

Mother of pearl is said to ease anger and aggression. It can be added to spells or amulets meant to calm a situation so rational discussion can take place. It helps reveal reasonable solutions to problems.

Peacock Ore

Peacock ore is a stone of social justice and equality. It's included in spells for moving on from trauma and stimulates independence and strength. This stone can be programmed to facilitate long-distance healing.

Pearl

Some witches believe pearls are bad luck because collecting them means killing living creatures. Doing so makes pearls useful in cursing, for those who practice that kind of witchcraft. Use your own intuition when deciding how you feel about pearls in your practice, or choose synthetic ones made from natural materials.

Peridot

Peridot attracts money and luck and dispels feelings of jealousy and envy. These properties can lessen the modern habit of comparing your own experience with the staged lives of others via social media. Keep some with your electronic device.

Petrified Wood

Petrified wood is from trees so ancient they've turned to stone. These stones are wise and contain the oldest knowledge of the earth, helping you understand the briefness of human life versus the wholeness of time. It's different from jet, because it's a solid brown rock and looks like wood grain.

Prehnite

Prehnite brings unconditional love for the self and others. It broadens your inner wisdom to guide you on your life's true purpose. It also enhances divination and psychic abilities.

Pumice

Pumice is unique because it floats on water, which means it can help you float above life's emotional difficulties while remaining strong. It cleanses the physical body and the aura at the same time.

Purpurite

Purpurite is a salesperson's stone. Whether you're running a large business, are self-employed, or are just having a garage sale, purpurite will enhance your products' appeal to customers and increase your revenue.

Quartz: Aqua Aura

This beguiling crystal is made by bonding gold with quartz, creating a mix of their energies. Gold is associated with the sun and riches, courage and will. Combined with quartz, this crystal makes a perfect self-empowerment amulet.

Quartz: Blue

Blue quartz brings peace and tranquility and is worn to lighten the spirits, alleviating bad moods. It welcomes hopeful feelings and dispels fear, and it's good to have when you're acting as a source of comfort for others.

Quartz: Golden

Golden quartz facilitates communication through telepathy and other psychic means. Visualize the person you wish to contact while whispering a message to golden quartz. It should carry your message to them.

Quartz: Green

Green quartz is a powerful beacon of prosperity. Carry it in your wallet to attract money, or keep a piece on your altar. It creates an aura of success around those who wear it.

Quartz: Lithium

Lithium quartz is healing for animals and foliage. Place it near plants that are ailing, or near the bed of a sick animal to aid their recovery.

Quartz: Phantom

The white wisp seen in phantom quartz is the ghost of the past and contains your previous lives. Phantom quartz serves to remind us of where we come from, how we grow from hardship, and what we've overcome.

Quartz: Rose

Rose quartz facilitates love in all its forms: love of self, of others, friendship, familial, and romantic. Rose quartz is used to encourage self-esteem, attract like-minded people, and find emotional connection.

Quartz: Smoky

Smoky quartz combats sadness and melancholy. It anchors you in reality while raising your vibration to open the way to contentment. It alleviates feelings of emptiness by filling you with life force. Smoky quartz can fade if it's left in the sun.

Quartz: Spirit

Spirit quartz encompasses all the powers of clear quartz and raises the vibration even higher. Keeping spirit quartz near someone who is transitioning from this life to the next will help them pass over peacefully.

Rhodochrosite

Rhodochrosite is a pink stone of physical attraction and lust. It encourages freedom of sexual expression and is included in spells to attract physical relationships and enhance sexual experiences.

Rhodonite

Rhodonite deflects insults and negative attention. If you believe someone is trying to damage your reputation, rhodonite can be added to spells for preventing the spread of rumors and lies.

Ruby

Rubies are associated with healthy gardens and crops, protecting them from storms and infestations. Touch a ruby to your favorite trees to guard them from harm and acknowledge the tree spirits inside them.

Sapphire

Sapphire can be included in spells for fidelity in love and understanding between partners. It's also believed to help avoid imprisonment and is used in rituals regarding legal matters. Sapphire will fade if it's left in direct sunlight.

Sardonyx

Sardonyx can be placed around a home to combat crime and theft. It brings out the best in people, helping make a good first impression. It's an excellent stone for community-building rituals.

Serpentine

Serpentine can be placed near the throat for those who have trouble communicating their thoughts. It can invoke a feeling of personal power, giving you the courage to discard what is no longer serving you, the way a snake sheds its skin.

Snowflake Obsidian

A gentler form of black obsidian, this glass can bring problems to the surface, to be dealt with when you're ready. It helps break unhealthy cycles of negativity.

Sodalite

Sodalite is an excellent communication stone. It brings solidarity to a group, allows people to share ideas, and encourages open communication. Associated with logic and intellect, it's a perfect stone for students.

Spinel

Spinel is for resetting and renewing yourself and things around you. It helps you let go of people and is useful in breakup spells. Spinel will attract new opportunities, putting you in the right place at the right time.

Sugilite

Sugilite acts as a magical shield in every way—emotionally, physically, and spiritually. It can bring love and light into the darkest of situations, so carry some with you while undergoing emotionally difficult experiences.

Super Seven

Named because it contains seven different minerals, this stone increases psychic ability, magical power, intuition, and your connection to Spirit all in one. It's excellent to work with when embarking on all spiritual pursuits.

Tiger Iron

Tiger iron encourages strength and resilience. It instills a sense of bravery when worn, making you stand behind your beliefs when they are challenged. It creates unwavering dedication to your values.

Topaz

Topaz attracts joy, abundance, and happiness. It spreads positive emotions from person to person like rays of sun. When you carry an empowered topaz, you'll noticeably brighten the energy everywhere you go. Do not cleanse it with salt, and avoid exposure to sunlight to prevent fading.

Tourmaline: Black

Black tourmaline protects the emotions of sensitive people and prevents empaths from becoming overwhelmed by the energy of others. Wear some in a crowd to create a shield around yourself.

Tourmaline: Blue

Blue tourmaline encourages truth, honesty, loyalty, and responsibility. Carry blue tourmaline when working with others, especially at a new job where you want to make a good impression.

Tourmaline: Brown

Brown tourmaline makes it easier for people to feel empathy. It encourages teamwork and is useful in healing arguments and dysfunction within families. It fosters understanding between people whose personalities clash.

Tourmaline: Green

Green tourmaline can help hone visualization skills, making it perfect for witchcraft and spell casting. It's especially attractive to witches who work with herbs, flowers, and plants.

Tourmaline: Pink

Pink tourmaline is an aphrodisiac used in love and sex magic. It can help a couple open up and be sexually comfortable with each other by dispelling insecurity around intimacy.

Tourmaline: Purple

Purple tourmaline gets rid of patterns that are no longer serving you. It can smooth out disordered thinking and combat self-imposed fear and insecurity.

Tourmaline: Rainbow

Rainbow tourmaline inspires creativity and enhances the imagination. It fights through writer's block and other creative obstructions, reaching deep down into the psyche to find the most unique ideas.

Tourmaline: Red

Red tourmaline can assist with overcoming shyness. It strengthens the will and helps with physical energy levels. For introverts, red tourmaline will keep their social battery charged in group situations.

Tourmaline: Watermelon

Watermelon tourmaline creates a feeling of balance and clarity, as it harmonizes contradicting traits within us. It also fosters gentleness between people and strengthens friendships.

Unakite

Unakite is the earth lover's stone. It resonates with those who love animals and nature. Unakite will strengthen the bond between a witch and their familiar animals.

Zircon

Clear zircon is a substitute for diamonds in spells and magic. Red zircon is for powerful sex magic, yellow aids business success, and orange keeps the home safe. Green zircon is excellent for money spells, and brown is for stability.

PART TWO

50 SPELLS, RITUALS, RITES, AND OTHER MAGICAL PRACTICES

Abundance and Prosperity

Money-Attraction Charm 92

Surprise Treasure Spell 93

Prosperity Powder 94

Prosperity Candle 95

Crystal Prosperity Amulet 96

Prosperity Crystal Grid 97

Protection and Clearing

Home-Protection Stones 99

Crystal Threshold Guardians 100

House-Cleansing/-Blessing Spray 101

Spell to Stop Gossip 102

Curse-Reversal Spell 103

Body, Mind, and Soul Protection Amulet 104

Pentacle Crystal Grid 105

Love and Relationships

Rose Quartz Attraction Spell 107

Spell to Heal a Relationship 108

Love-Attracting Elixir 109

Larimar Soul Mate Spell 110

Lodestone Relationship Strengthener 111

Crystal Grid for Love 112

Creativity and Manifestation

Go with the Flow Pumice Spell 114

Road-Opener Oil 115

Creativity Candle Spell 116

Malachite to Destroy Creative Blockages 117

All-Purpose Manifestation Spell 118

Doubt-Destroyer Soap 119

Divination and Spiritual Awakening

Connecting to the Astral Realm 120

Psychic Friends 121

Crystal Oracle 122

Awaken and Grow Spell 123

Past Life Recall Bracelet 124

Ammolite Witch Bath 125

Self-Care and Emotional Healing

Spell to Remove Sadness 127

Spell to Release the Past 128

Mica Mindfulness
Meditation 129

Social Media Talisman 131

Social Battery Charger 132

Peaceful-Atmosphere Spell 133

Physical Health and Wellness

Crystal Grid for Health 135

Witch Bottle for Wellness 136

Iolite Habit Breaker 137

Green Jasper Tea 138

Boji Stones Balancing
Meditation 140

Healing Witch Doll 141

Ceremonial Rites and Celebrations

Samhain: Messages
from the Dead 142

Yule: Yule Tree Crystals 143

Imbolc: Knot Magic
Ceremony 145

Ostara/Spring Equinox:
Ostara Gifts of Divination 146

Beltane/May Day: Dew
and Fire Ritual 148

Litha/Summer Solstice:
Honoring the Flowers 149

Lughnasadh: Gratitude for
the Earth Ritual 151

Mabon/Fall Equinox:
Welcoming the Darkness 152

MONEY-ATTRACTION CHARM

This spell involves creating a money-drawing charm. Keep the charm in your house, your place of work, or in your wallet to bring a boost of prosperous energy to your life.

> 1 stick incense
> 1 circle green or golden cloth, about 7 inches in diameter
> 1 small citrine crystal
> 4 coins
> 1 cinnamon stick
> 1 foot green or gold ribbon

1. Gather all your materials on your altar and light a stick of incense. One at a time, pass each item through the smoke to cleanse them.
2. Lay out the cloth circle and place the citrine in its center. Imagine it surrounded by golden light the color of the sun.
3. Place the coins in your palm. Close your eyes and imagine them growing in number, multiplying until thousands of coins are spilling out of your hand like a waterfall.
4. Place one coin on the cloth next to the citrine. Say, *One to bring it.*
5. Place the second coin on the cloth and say, *Two to make it grow.*
6. Place the third coin on the cloth and say, *Three to keep it.*
7. Place the fourth coin on the cloth and say, *Four to help it flow.*
8. Put the cinnamon stick on the cloth with the other materials. Cinnamon has a fiery energy and it acts as a spark to ignite the spell.
9. Hold your palms above the gathered items and feel the combined energy they're emitting: prosperity, growth, and success. Visualize your goal as you want it to be. See yourself paying off bills, going on vacation, or whatever financial need you may have.
10. Tie up the cloth using the ribbon, creating a little bag.
11. Hang the bag somewhere or stash it in a secret place to attract money.

This spell is best performed during the waxing moon, but can be done any time you're in need. Once your money has manifested, cleanse the materials and reuse them in another spell.

SURPRISE TREASURE SPELL

Moss agate is known for uncovering wealth in unexpected places. This spell will create an amulet to help attract this kind of luck by chance, to increase your odds of winning or finding money when you least expect it. Perform this spell during the full moon.

 1 moss agate stone
 Pen
 8-by-11-inch piece of paper
 1 glass jar with a lid
 1 cup soil from a healthy garden or vegetable patch

1. Gather all your materials on your altar. Make sure you have already cleansed, charged, and empowered your moss agate stone.
2. Using your pen, draw your lucky numbers or personal symbols on the paper, filling the page with whatever you like. If you're unsure what to sketch, some suggestions are dollar signs, coins, the sun, and pentacles. Don't worry about how it looks; it's your intent that is important. While you sketch, visualize yourself winning money. Imagine exactly how surprised and happy you'll feel.
3. Place the moss agate on the paper and fold it up as small as possible. The moss agate will absorb the energy you put into your lucky symbols.
4. Put the folded paper in the jar and cover it with earth, as if you're planting a seed. The earth is fertile and rich—perfect qualities to create growth and abundance.
5. Screw the lid on the jar, and leave it sitting on a windowsill or outdoors overnight to bask in the power of the full moon.
6. The next day, retrieve your moss agate stone. Burn or recycle the paper. The stone now holds all the energy of your lucky symbols and the fertility of the earth.

Carry your moss agate with you when you go to a casino or play the lottery or any game of chance. It's also useful to carry it when you need some cash in general, to increase your odds of finding the money you need.

PROSPERITY POWDER

Magical powders can be made for any purpose and are wonderfully versatile. Sprinkle this prosperity powder around the edges of your home or business to attract money. You can also burn some on a charcoal disk like incense, rub it between your fingers, or add a pinch to your potted plants or garden. This prosperity powder is crafted from crystals and herbs chosen for their associations with prosperity.

> 1 part crushed pyrite, cleansed, charged, and empowered
>   with prosperity
> 1 part dried peppermint
> 1 part dried cloves
> 1 part dried sage
> Mortar and pestle
> Glass jar with a lid
> 1 small tigereye stone

1. Cleanse, charge, and empower your pyrite with prosperity powers.
2. Gather your materials on your altar.
3. Place your crushed pyrite and dried peppermint, cloves, and sage in your mortar and pestle. As you put your physical energy into crushing and grinding the mixture, imagine it glowing brighter and brighter with a green aura. When the ingredients become a coarse powder, transfer them to the jar.
4. Take the tigereye stone in your hand and contemplate its energy. Think of it as a money-drawing magnet. Hold the tigereye in front of your mouth where your breath will reach it. Whisper,

Prosperity and abundance
Are on their way to me
Anchored with stability
Like the roots of a tree.
Flourishing with fruitfulness
Blooming all around
All the money that I need
Can easily be found.

5. Place the tigereye in the powder. Close the lid and shake it up.
6. Use this powder as needed. When it's all gone, reuse the jar and cleanse the tigereye.

If you don't have crushed pyrite pieces, you can easily make your own. Hold a piece of pyrite to your heart and surround it with love to communicate that your actions come from a benevolent place. Then place the pyrite in a sturdy bag, lay it on a hard surface like cement or a rock, and tap it with a hammer.

PROSPERITY CANDLE

Candle magic is part of many witchcraft workings. A spell candle can incorporate crystals, herbs, oils, and color magic based on the intention of the witch. Since most candles take many hours to burn, some candle spells take place over a series of days, reaffirming your intention every time you light the wick. This prosperity candle spell is best started the day after the new moon and continued for the duration of the waxing moon phase.

3 small pieces green quartz
3 drops diluted patchouli oil (5 drops of patchouli essential oil diluted in 1 ounce of jojoba oil)
1 unscented green votive candle
1 plate to catch candle drippings
2 tablespoons dried clover

1. Empower the green quartz pieces with your intention to attract wealth.
2. Put a few drops of diluted patchouli oil on your fingers, then rub the oil all over the surface of the candle. Imagine the candle surrounded by golden light. The scent of patchouli is associated with earthly delights, material gain, and tangible experiences.
3. Set the candle on the plate and place the 3 green quartz crystals on top of it, around the wick, pointing outward.
4. Surround the base of the candle with the dried clover. Clover is a symbol of luck.
5. Light the candle and spend at least 10 minutes visualizing yourself and your loved ones achieving your goal, enjoying abundance and wealth in a way that's suited to you. Your intention flows from your forehead, into the flame, and then is sent out in all directions,

amplified by the golden fire and the quartz crystals. The light of the flame carries your desire to Spirit.

6. Light the candle at the same time each day and repeat the visualization until the candle burns itself out, preferably near the full moon.

7. When the spell is complete and the candle has burned all the way down, you can remove the stones from the wax and carry them with you to attract wealth everywhere you go.

As the candle burns, the quartz will become imbedded in the wax, and eventually a puddle of wax and herbs will form on the plate. Be sure to examine the shapes in the dried remains for symbols and omens. For a comprehensive list of symbolism in divination, visit the symbol dictionary at DivinationbyTeaLeaves.com. Although this website focuses on reading tea leaves, the meaning of the symbols is universal.

CRYSTAL PROSPERITY AMULET

A magical amulet is any object that a witch has empowered to attract or repel a specific thing. The object is filled with condensed energy that emits a focused vibration, which then manifests your intention. This wealth-amplifying amulet is meant to be carried in your wallet or placed near where you keep your money.

> 1 quartz point
> 1 golden candle
> Pen
> Piece of paper, no bigger than paper money
> Paper money bill

1. Cleanse, charge, and empower your quartz point with amplification powers.

2. Gather your materials at your altar or in a sacred space and light the golden candle.

3. Using your pen and paper, make a very specific list of the things you need to buy or pay for at this time. This may be bills you need to pay off, a material object you've been wishing for, or any personal goal.

4. Lay the money on your altar and place your list on top of it.

5. Take your quartz point and put it on top of the list and the money. Imagine it drawing up the energy of the money and your intentions, and then amplifying them outward in a burst of golden shimmering light. See this light reaching all the way up to the sky and the universe beyond. Visualize the one bill turning into many bills, thousands of bills. Imagine your bank account statement with the number you wish to see.
6. Say, *This crystal amplifies and multiplies everything it touches. This is my will, so mote it be.*
7. Roll the bill around the list and crystal. Using your golden candle, drip wax onto the bill to seal it closed. You may wish to drip wax into the ends of the tube to keep the crystal intact as well.
8. Carry the charm with you until your needs have manifested. Afterward, take it apart, cleanse the crystal, and bury the bill.

"So mote it be" is a phrase commonly used in spells to declare your will to Spirit.

PROSPERITY CRYSTAL GRID

This crystal grid follows the Seed of Life pattern, shown on page 98. You can trace it out on paper or buy a template from a metaphysical shop. The Seed of Life is exactly that: a thought that grows into a material life form. Using it as a base for your grid ensures the growth and manifestation of your intention.

> 1 large quartz point
> 6 small quartz points
> 6 pieces jade
> 6 chunks pyrite
> 1 Seed of Life grid template
> 1 paper money bill, a special coin, or your intentions written on a small piece of paper and folded
> Wand or athame

1. Empower each of the crystals with prosperity and money-attracting energy.
2. Place the grid template on a flat surface. Put your money or folded paper in the center of the Seed of Life. Place your large quartz point on top of it. This quartz is the Master Stone and will draw

together the energy of all the other crystals and your intention to amplify their power.

3. At the center of the grid is what looks like a flower with 6 petals. Gather your 6 small quartz points and place one in each of these innermost petals, facing inward. These are your Way Stones and will direct energy from your prosperity crystals into the Master Stone.

4. Place your 6 pieces of jade in the next ring of circles.

5. Finally, evenly space your pyrite pieces around the outer circle of the grid. The jade and pyrite are your Desire Stones.

6. Using your wand or athame, trace the lines of the Seed of Life repeatedly while visualizing yourself gaining prosperity. Be sure to connect all the crystals with the movement of your wand. As you connect them, feel the energy of the grid becoming stronger.

7. Leave the grid in place as long as necessary.

As you become more experienced with crystal grids, you can create more complicated versions of this spell. Some witches integrate flower petals and herbs into their grids, or lay their patterns out intuitively rather than following a template.

Prosperity Crystal Grid

HOME-PROTECTION STONES

Placing empowered crystals around the perimeter of your home will create a protective barrier around your space and your loved ones. If you have a yard, you can bury the stones around the edges. If you live in an apartment, place them in the outermost corners of your living space.

4 black agate stones
4 teaspoons dried rosemary
4 teaspoons salt
1 bowl

1. Cleanse, charge, and empower your stones with protective energy.
2. Put the rosemary and the salt together in the bowl and mix them thoroughly with your fingers. While you do so, envision protective black energy flowing from your fingertips into the mixture.
3. Add the black agate stones to the bowl and mix them in.
4. Go to the east-facing wall or area of your property. Say, *I call upon the east, spirits of air. Guard and protect this space.* Bury one stone in the ground if you're outdoors. If you're inside, place it on the floor.
5. Now, walking clockwise, move toward the south. As you do, sprinkle salt and rosemary along the floor or ground and imagine it creating a thick protective barrier. Face the south and say, *I call upon the south, spirits of fire. Guard and protect this space.* Bury or place the next stone.
6. Continue to the west, walking clockwise and sprinkling salt and rosemary. Leave a stone as you say, *I call upon the west, spirits of water. Guard and protect this space.*
7. Continue to the north, sprinkling salt and rosemary. Place the last stone appropriately and say, *I call upon the north, spirits of earth. Guard and protect this space.*
8. Sprinkle salt and rosemary as you continue on to the east, completing the circle.

9. Visualize a strong, opaque barrier of black energy coming from the salt and rosemary circle. The stones connect the protective energy and stabilize it over your space, keeping it there even after the salt has been washed away.
10. Repeat once a month or as necessary.

If you've done this ritual indoors, you can vacuum up the salt and rosemary after an hour or so. It will leave its residual protective energy behind.

CRYSTAL THRESHOLD GUARDIANS

Some crystals are especially excellent at purifying the energy of everyone they come near. This spell creates an energetic filter that ensures those who enter your home or room will leave their negativity at the door. It clears away bad vibes, clouds of gloom, and unwanted entities.

> 2 quartz crystals
> 2 kunzite crystals
> 2 pieces selenite
> 2 aquamarine crystals
> 2 bowls
> Sand to fill the bowls, preferably from a beach or other watery area
> 2 white candles

1. Make sure all your crystals are empowered with the intention to cleanse and purify.
2. Fill the bowls with sand. Securely place a white candle in each bowl by pressing it upright into the sand. Add one piece of quartz, kunzite, selenite, and aquamarine to each bowl, arranged around the candle.
3. Place a bowl on each side of your main doorway.
4. Open the door wide. Light the candles and sit in the threshold.
5. Enter a meditative state and imagine the cleansing energy of the crystals moving up the candles and into the flames, and then filling up the doorway with light. Visualize the warm glow as it completely fills the rectangular space of the door, creating a film that swirls with the colors of the crystals.

6. Using your finger (or a wand or athame, if you prefer), draw a pentacle in the air in front of you, right in the doorway. Say, *By stones and by flame, by water and by air, I create a shield in this space and time. No evil or unwanted energy may enter here.*
7. Continue to visualize the shield until your attention wavers. Blow out the candles.

The sand will absorb and ground any negativity that is siphoned off from your guests. Once a week, light the candles and repeat the spell. When the candles burn all the way down, cleanse your crystals and replace the sand and candles.

HOUSE-CLEANSING/ -BLESSING SPRAY

Cleansing and blessing room sprays are a popular replacement for smoldering plants during smoke ceremonies, especially for those with sensitive lungs or who simply dislike the smell of burning herbs. These sprays are easy to make yourself and just as effective. If possible, use rainwater for an extra boost of natural purification.

1 part dried sage
1 part dried lavender
1 part dried rose petals or buds
2 parts water
1 spray bottle
1 or more rainbow fluorite crystals
Pinch salt

1. Put the sage, lavender, rose petals, and water in a pot. Bring to a boil on the stove, then lower the heat and simmer gently for 10 minutes. Allow to cool completely, and then strain. Fill your spray bottle with the potion.
2. Bring your materials to your altar and place them before you.
3. Hold the rainbow fluorite crystal(s) in your hand. This multicolored crystal contains the powers of prosperity, wisdom, purification, and many blessings all in one. Imagine your home or space exactly as you wish it to be: harmonious, peaceful, and blessed.

4. Place one or more stones in the spray bottle. As you do so, imagine the bottle lighting up from within with a mystical glow.
5. Add a pinch of salt to the bottle as a spiritual cleansing agent. Close the lid and shake it up.
6. Whenever you need to, spray your entire home with the potion to bring purity and blessings. As you do so, visualize every corner and crevice being filled with sparkling magical energy.

This potion is best made in a batch during the full moon. If you prefer a more aromatic spray, you can use essential oils instead of making a brew. In that case, simply fill your bottle with water, add about 5 drops each of sage, lavender, and rose oil (or rose water, as real rose oil is very expensive), instead of boiling the plants.

SPELL TO STOP GOSSIP

Gossip and wagging tongues can cause far-spreading damage in your personal and business life. This spell is meant to halt harmful gossip or lies against you or someone you care about, providing protection against further slander. This working goes straight to the source of the lies and stops them.

1 beryl crystal
Wax paper or tray
1 black candle
1 lump of modeling clay, slightly larger than your beryl crystal
7 pins

1. Empower your beryl crystal to avert gossip.
2. Gather your items on your altar. You'll be working with modeling clay, so lay out some wax paper or a tray to protect your altar from any mess.
3. Light the black candle.
4. Mold the clay into a ball while visualizing the person who is doing the gossiping. Imagine their physical appearance, the sound of their voice, and their mannerisms. Now, press your thumb into the ball of clay, creating an indent large enough to place your beryl crystal inside it. This hole represents their mouth. If you're artistic, you can mold the clay to look like lips, but this isn't absolutely necessary.

5. While holding the clay, picture them saying harmful things about you. In your mind, see their mouth moving. Take your beryl crystal and stuff it into the hole you made in the clay, symbolically cutting off their words.
6. Press the edges of the clay over the beryl, covering it completely, like lips closing.
7. Insert each pin through the clay seam over the crystal, as if closing two lips over the stone. As you push each pin through, say out loud, (Name), *you are rendered silent. No one hears your lies.*
8. Leave the charm somewhere it will not be disturbed until the problem has passed. You can then cleanse and reuse your beryl for other purposes.

This spell will not physically stop a person from speaking, but it will negate the effectiveness of their gossip and lies. Soon they'll stop spreading rumors because their words are ineffectual.

CURSE-REVERSAL SPELL

You don't have to know a whole coven of witches to feel like you've been cursed. Although it's quite possible that someone has sent baneful magic your way, you can also perform this spell when you're just having a run of particularly bad luck or when you feel especially targeted by someone else's negative feelings.

1 black onyx stone
1 stick incense
Small mirror
Handheld fan

1. If possible, take your materials to an outdoor place where you will not be disturbed.
2. Empower your onyx with the ability to turn back curses and ill will.
3. Sit comfortably and place the onyx in front of you. Notice its dark, mysterious surface, and visualize its deflective energy, how it repels all vibrations sent at it. It will be sitting with you during this spell to add its curse-stopping power to your working.
4. Light your stick of incense and secure it in the ground or in a holder between yourself and the onyx.

5. Face the mirror away from you, so it reflects the smoke of the incense. You can do this by leaning it against something or propping it up in the dirt. This mirror is reflecting all light and energy away from it and therefore away from you.

6. Using your fan, begin to waft the incense smoke away from you. Say, *As I send this smoke away, I send away all curses. Evil be gone.*

7. Burn the entire stick of incense while continuously fanning the smoke away. The smoke represents the curse, and you are returning it to the sender.

8. Throughout the spell, be aware of the black onyx and the protective energy it's emitting. You'll notice the smoke doesn't seem to touch the stone, as the onyx repels the curse that the smoke represents.

9. When the incense burns out, gather your onyx and mirror and walk away from the area, knowing you've averted the curse.

Carry your onyx with you or place it on a windowsill of your home until you feel the curse has been lifted. If you have to do this spell indoors, be sure to open a window.

BODY, MIND, AND SOUL PROTECTION AMULET

The simplest form of crystal protection magic is to empower several complementary protective crystals, keep them in a small bag, and wear them around your neck. You can buy an aesthetically pleasing bag for crystals in many shops or make your own. This working creates a wearable amulet that will provide protection for body, mind, and soul.

1 white candle
1 small agate
1 small chalcedony
1 small amethyst
1 small bag on a cord that can be worn around your neck

1. Gather your materials at your altar. Light the white candle.

2. Hold the agate to your heart and feel its energy protecting your physical self. Whisper to the stone, *This stone will protect my body.* Place it on the altar.

3. Hold the chalcedony to your heart, feeling its intellectually stimulating vibrations. Whisper to the stone, *This stone will protect my mind.*
4. Hold the amethyst to your heart, feeling its power to shield your spirit. Whisper to the crystal, *This stone will protect my spirit.*
5. Place them all in the bag. Visualize their energy mingling into one powerful swirling ball of colorful light. Put the necklace over your head and feel the power of the stones spreading all over your body in a shield of swirling color. This shield spreads about 3 feet out from your physical self. It encompasses your entire aura.
6. Wear this amulet as needed to protect your mind, body, and spirit.

These three crystals form a perfect triplet of protection in amulet form. Together, they guard against physical illness, mental manipulation, and unwanted entities latching onto your spirit.

PENTACLE CRYSTAL GRID

The pentacle, or five-pointed star within a circle, is a powerful symbol in many witchcraft practices. This protection crystal grid is based on the shape of the pentacle. You can build this grid on your altar to guard you during magical workings or place it elsewhere in the home for a general shield against unwanted forces.

Pentacle template, or a flat disk featuring a pentacle
1 large black tourmaline
5 small quartz points
5 small pieces flint
Athame or wand

1. Find a spot to make your grid that will not be disturbed by people or animals.
2. Empower each of the crystals you'll be using with protective energy.
3. Lay the pentacle on a flat surface.
4. Place the large black tourmaline in the center of the pentacle. This is the Master Stone.

5. One by one, place the quartz pieces within the points of the star, with their points facing the black tourmaline. These are Way Stones.
6. On each point of the star, put a piece of flint. These are Desire Stones.
7. Using your wand or athame, trace an invisible line in the air above the crystals, joining them all and creating the shape of a star. Then move your wand or athame around the circle clockwise, joining them all together.
8. Spend some time visualizing the protective aura the grid is creating. There will be a cone of power coming from the pentacle, drawing energy up and condensing it above the symbol in a point. This point reaches all the way into the sky and disappears into the spirit realm.
9. Every time you see the grid, feel its protective energy. Acknowledging it will continue to feed it, making it more powerful over time.

The pentacle can be used for crystal grids for almost any witchy intention, including prosperity, love, and peace. Although the pentacle is not a popular form of sacred geometry, it's a powerful symbol that has gained meaning in the collective unconscious for many years.

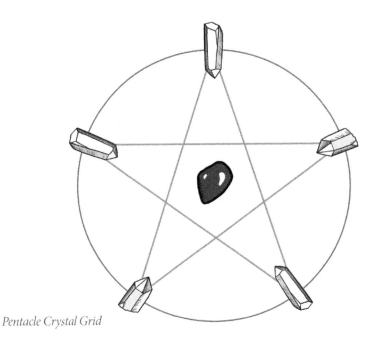

Pentacle Crystal Grid

ROSE QUARTZ ATTRACTION SPELL

This is a spell to attract a romantic relationship into your life. It's not meant to target a specific individual, but rather puts trust in Spirit to connect you with the right person. The spell should begin on the first night of the waxing moon and be completed on the full moon.

> 2 rose quartz crystals
> 1 pink or red candle
> Dried rose petals

1. Gather your materials on your altar.
2. One rose quartz represents you, and the other represents the kind of person you wish to attract. Decide which stone is which.
3. Place the stone representing your mate against your heart, and visualize the traits you wish to attract in a partner. Feel free to go into full fantasy mode; this is your chance to really declare what you want.
4. Place the rose quartz crystals 14 inches apart on your altar and light the candle.
5. Visualize yourself meeting and developing a relationship with the person you desire, and as you do so, move the stones toward each other about 1 inch. Blow out the candle.
6. The next day, and every day after for the remainder of the waxing moon, light the candle and repeat the visualization around the same time. Spend about 10 minutes imagining your goal as if you already have it, seeing yourself and a partner in a happy relationship. While visualizing, move the stones 1 inch closer together.
7. On the full moon, your stones should be touching each other. Sprinkle the dried rose petals all over them and declare to Spirit, *My partner is on their way to me. As I will it, so mote it be.* Allow the candle to burn all the way down.

8. Leave the petals and crystals on the altar and keep your eyes and mind open for potential partners.

Many witches believe performing love spells that target a specific person is unethical, as it interferes with the other person's free will. This spell doesn't name an individual, but opens your eyes to all the possibilities and attracts people best suited to you. Be open-minded during this time—your partner may be someone you least expect!

SPELL TO HEAL A RELATIONSHIP

This spell will help heal a relationship that has been through difficulty, where one or more parties have been wounded but both of you still want to forgive and stay together. Before performing this spell, do some meditation to ensure that this is indeed a positive relationship that is healthy for everyone involved.

> 2 rhodonite crystals
> 2 pieces of paper
> Colored pencils or markers, including red
> Scissors
> Tape

1. Empower the crystals with emotional healing energy before you begin.
2. At your altar, draw a picture of your partner on one piece of paper, and on the other a picture of yourself. They don't have to be artistic or drawn perfectly; it's the intention that's important. Be sure to include features of the person such as hair color, body shape, or tattoos. Cut the figures out with scissors and lay them side by side.
3. Draw a heart in each figure's chest and color them red. These hearts represent the wound between you. As you draw and color the hearts, consider what has happened and the pain it has caused.
4. Set a rhodonite crystal over your partner's heart, while imagining the crystal drawing the pain out of them. Repeat this with the figure of yourself.
5. Let the figures sit overnight with the crystals on their hearts to heal them.

6. The next day, remove the rhodonite. Press the paper figures face-to-face and tape them together. This signifies the two of you reuniting pain-free.

7. Let the papers sit undisturbed. Give one rhodonite to your partner and keep the other for yourself.

8. As you both carry the rhodonite for a period of time, you should discover yourselves overcoming the problem and finding ways to move on.

This spell can't change the past, but it will encourage new understanding and forgiveness to enter your hearts, so your relationship can heal and move forward.

LOVE-ATTRACTING ELIXIR

Elixirs are a well-known way to transfer the energy of a crystal into water, which is then drunk to fill the body with that same energy. Elixirs can be made to match almost any intention, depending on what crystals you have and whether they're safe to put in water. Here is a recipe for a love-attracting elixir.

Glass bowl
Drinking water
1 or more jade, pink agate, rose quartz, or pink jasper

1. During the full moon, fill the bowl with drinking water.

2. Empower your crystals for love. Each one has a slightly different vibration. Jade brings long-lasting love, pink agate brings a stable emotional attachment, rose quartz brings the giddiness that comes with meeting a new love interest, and pink jasper attracts a strong, mature bond.

3. If you're using more than one crystal, add them to the water one at a time. Put one crystal in and imagine its energy filling up the water with light while visualizing yourself attracting the perfect relationship. Remove it after about 5 minutes. Go on to the next crystal and repeat, until you have infused the water with each of the different stones you wish to use.

4. Transfer the water to a glass or bottle. Whenever you drink some of the water, imagine the energy of the love-attracting crystals coursing through your veins and heart, making you glow with

attraction energy. This energy is like a magnet, drawing in all kinds of love to you.

To dilute your elixir, add several drops of the elixir to your drinking water instead of drinking it directly. Alternatively, add the elixir to your bathwater, anoint your pulse points, or sprinkle it in your sacred space. If you choose to add other crystals, make absolutely certain they are not toxic.

LARIMAR SOUL MATE SPELL

A soul mate is typically thought of as a life-long partner. But sometimes a soul mate is a person who is pivotal in your life's path—a meaningful but temporary connection from which you learn valuable life lessons. Soul mates can take many forms, and we can have more than one in our lifetime, so be open-minded about what or who comes your way.

1 larimar crystal, preferably a pendant that can be worn as
    a necklace
Lavender oil
1 chain or cord the length of a necklace
1 heart charm

1. Empower your larimar to attract a soul mate. Gather your materials on your altar.
2. Place a drop of lavender oil on the larimar and rub it in. Imagine the larimar acting as a searchlight, reaching out into the universe and calling to your soul mate. String it onto the cord or chain.
3. Place a drop of lavender oil on the heart charm and as you rub it into the heart, visualize yourself spending time with your soul mate, however that looks for you. Feel your own heart expanding with love and connection. Say, *I call to the heart of my soul mate. Come and find me now.* String it onto the chain.
4. The larimar and the heart are now together, touching each other. This represents the union of you and your soul mate.
5. Wear the necklace. Every seven days, anoint the stone and heart with lavender oil while visualizing your relationship with your soul mate.

This spell is best done during the waxing or full moon. Larimar crystal pendants are available from many online shops, or you can make a pendant from a loose larimar stone and jewelry-maker's wire.

LODESTONE RELATIONSHIP STRENGTHENER

Lodestone, or magnetite, is one of the only naturally occurring magnets found on earth. This spell is to strengthen the bond between you and your partner. It will fortify your relationship if you are going through a rough patch or when you must be physically parted for a length of time.

2 medium lodestones
Bowl of ordinary rocks or pebbles found outdoors
1 foot red yarn or string

1. Decide which lodestone represents you and which one represents your partner. To empower the lodestone that represents you, you can simply carry it for a day or sleep with it under your pillow to absorb your energy.
2. Gather your materials at your altar. Pick up the stone that represents your partner. Hold it close to your heart and visualize their face, voice, and all the qualities you love about them. Send this imagery from your heart into the stone.
3. Hold the bowl of pebbles up to the sky. Say, *Powers of earth, stability, and protection, I invoke you to aid me in my working. These rocks are a source of safety, security, nurturance, and growth.* Visualize the rocks glowing with gentle brown and green light. Set the bowl aside.
4. Hold one lodestone in each hand. Slowly bring them together and as they touch, really feel the magnetic connection that is holding them together. That is your love. Wrap the string around them and tie it in a bow, binding them together.
5. Gently place the charm in the bowl of rocks. As you adjust the stones and pebbles to cover the charm, imagine you're gently tucking it into a safe, protected place.
6. Place this bowl somewhere safe until the rough patch has passed.

After the difficult time is over, recover your lodestones from the bowl. You can keep them tied together like this as a relationship amulet or undo them and cleanse the stones to be reused.

CRYSTAL GRID FOR LOVE

This crystal grid can be made anywhere in your home, or if you're in an existing relationship, carefully placed beneath the bed you share with your partner to strengthen your bond. The Flower of Life grid is made up of 19 circles, each containing a flower with six petals. It's on each of these overlapping flowers that you'll place your crystals.

> Flower of Life grid template
> 1 red rose petal, or your intention written on paper and folded up small
> 1 large quartz point
> 6 small quartz points
> 6 rose quartz crystals
> 6 garnet stones
> Athame or wand

1. Place your rose petal or intention in the center flower of the grid and place the large quartz point on top of it. This is your Master Stone. If you're using a rose petal, be aware that it's sending out a high frequency of love and attraction due to its history of being one of the most romantic symbols.
2. Add your small quartz points to the six flowers around the Master Stone on the grid, pointing outward, evenly spaced. These are your Way Stones.
3. Add your rose quartz crystals to the next row of six circles around the quartz points.
4. Place your garnet stones on the outermost circles. The garnet and the rose quartz are your Desire Stones.
5. You should have a stone inside each of the 19 circles in the Flower of Life grid, all evenly spaced.
6. Using your wand or athame, energetically connect the stones by tracing the symbol of the Flower of Life in the air above the grid, being sure to join all the stones. While you do this, visualize exactly the kind of relationship or love you wish for.

This crystal grid uses a combination of garnet and rose quartz as Desire Stones. Garnet brings a physical, sexual energy to the grid, which is tempered by the emotional, gentle power of the rose quartz crystal.

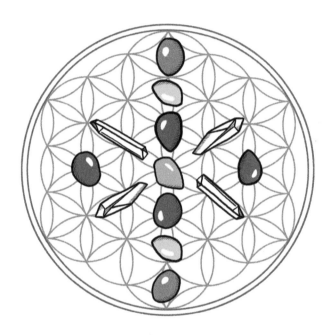

Crystal Grid for Love

GO WITH THE FLOW PUMICE SPELL

Sometimes the most challenging part of creativity and manifestation is relinquishing control and allowing your purpose to unfold as it's meant to. We find ourselves demanding outcomes or rushing things, which always ends in frustration. This spell is to help you go with the natural flow of Spirit and learn to trust that you will fulfill your destiny. You'll need access to a lake, river, stream, or pond, as this spell calls upon the energy of water.

1 small pumice stone
3 drops of your favorite essential oil

1. Cleanse, charge, and empower your pumice stone to absorb energy.
2. Gather your materials and find a spot to sit by the water where you won't be disturbed. Hold the pumice stone in your hand.
3. Be aware of the gentle, undulating energy of the water. Notice how it flows exactly as it needs to, with no hurry or stress.
4. Examine the pumice stone in your palm. Imagine your frustration and stress gathering in your forehead. Visualize this energy streaming from your head into the stone. It may look like a torrent of confused and chaotic scribbles.
5. Place three drops of your chosen oil onto the stone. Doing so joins the stone to you personally, so that no matter where its energy flows, it will carry your stress away with it.
6. Place your fingertips in the water, if possible. Ask the water to teach you how to flow with nature, uninhibited, calmly and openly accepting whatever comes. The water doesn't judge where it goes or what it picks up; it simply keeps going at its own pace and in its own way. These are the qualities you want to share with the water.
7. Toss your pumice stone into the water to drift away, taking your chaotic, stressed thoughts with it.

Pumice will float in the water, easily and carelessly going wherever the current takes it. Walk away. You'll soon find that your creativity is flowing, natural and free, opening the way to manifesting your dreams.

ROAD-OPENER OIL

As its name suggests, this magical oil is meant to create openings and opportunities and to clear the way for manifestation of all kinds. It can be used to anoint candles or your pulse points, added to magical baths, and more. The recipe draws on the ancient Egyptian belief that bloodstone can detect openings and break down walls.

1 bloodstone
1 small jar with a lid
1 small piece gingerroot
A few leaves fresh lemon balm, or 1 teaspoon dried lemon balm
3 drops tea tree oil
Olive or jojoba oil to fill the jar

1. Gather your materials at your altar on the full moon.
2. Hold your bloodstone up to the moon and say, *Bloodstone is the magic key that opens doors to opportunity*. Place the stone in the jar.
3. Hold the gingerroot up to the moon and say, *Ginger's heat to light the fire, which clears the way to my desires*. Place it in the jar.
4. Hold the lemon balm up to the moon and say, *This little bit of lemon balm will bring success and keep me strong*. Add the lemon balm to the jar.
5. Add three drops of tea tree oil to the mix and say, *Cleansing oils to wash away all opposition in my way*.
6. Fill the jar with jojoba or olive oil.
7. Gently shake the jar and observe the ingredients and their powers mingling in a swirl of potent energy. Visualize an image of gates blowing open to reveal a wide, sunny road leading into the horizon. This is the road to your success. Send this thought into the oil through your hands.
8. Let the oil sit in the sun for three days and then strain it.

Every time you use this oil, envision the path to your goals and dreams opening up before you like a wide, unobstructed road with nobody on it but you. Visualize achieving your goals easily and naturally.

CREATIVITY CANDLE SPELL

This spell is meant to inspire creativity to manifest any project. It's useful for writing, the arts, teaching, learning, or doing business; things that require new ideas, an open mind, and a willingness to take risks. Perform this spell where you do your creative work.

    1 chrysoprase crystal
    1 red taper candle
    1 yellow taper candle
    1 orange taper candle
    3 drops tangerine or orange essential oil, diluted in a carrier oil
        (5 drops essential oil per ounce of jojoba or almond oil)
    3 candleholders
    Salt

1. Empower your chrysoprase crystal with creativity.
2. Anoint each of the candles with the oil while visualizing creativity flooding into your space. Starting at the wick, rub the oil toward the middle of the candle. Then rub the oil from the bottom of the candle to the middle. This is a drawing or attracting motion used in candle magic.
3. Place the candles in holders in a small circle.
4. Put your chrysoprase crystal in the center of the circle of candles.
5. Make a circle of salt around the candles. This marks the space as sacred and protects their power for the duration of the spell.
6. Light the candles, knowing you're lighting the fire of your own creativity.
7. Visualize the warmth of the flames heating up the chrysoprase, igniting its creative powers all around you and inside of you. Imagine the room coming alive with flashes of creative energy. When you're finished, blow the candles out.
8. Every time you enter your workspace, light the candles and visualize this same thing before you begin work. Blow the candles out at the end of each day.

Once the candles are burned all the way down, cleanse your chrysoprase and repeat the spell with new candles and fresh salt. Only perform this ritual where it's safe to light candles.

MALACHITE TO DESTROY CREATIVE BLOCKAGES

Malachite is a perfect stone for destroying mental and creative blockages, allowing new information and ideas to come through. Eyebright is an herb for opening your inner eye, which helps with creation and manifestation. This charm can be used again and again, any time you feel your ability to manifest your magic is being impeded in some way.

> 1 malachite stone
> 1 clear plastic fillable ball ornament, found in craft stores
> Sand to fill the ball
> 1 teaspoon ground eyebright herb
> Glue

1. Empower the malachite stone with the ability to smash mental and creative blockages.
2. Gather your items at your altar.
3. Fill the ball with sand. Imagine the ball represents your mind and your thoughts, and the sand is your ideas, magical abilities, and creativity.
4. Add the eyebright to the ball.
5. Place the malachite inside the ball and glue the ball closed.
6. Roll the ball around and watch as the malachite stone cuts through the sand, opening new pathways and moving all the granules around in fresh, unique ways.
7. Place the ball on your altar and hold the palms of your hands above it. Feel the heat and energy of your hands transferring into the charm. Say, *Eyebright herb and stone of green, open my inner eye, cutting through all blockages, so my magical powers fly.*
8. Anytime you feel blocked creatively or your magic isn't manifesting, shake the ball, observe the malachite changing the shape of the sand, and say the rhyme. For meditation, slowly turn the ball and watch the stone make paths through the sand to sooth and inspire.

If you can't find a craft ball, a transparent jar or bottle with a tight lid will do. If you're feeling especially blocked, try creating this charm on the new or dark moon. The dynamic energy present may lend this working an extra boost of power.

ALL-PURPOSE MANIFESTATION SPELL

This spell is to manifest any need or desire you have in your life at this moment. This can be something either material or intangible; if you can imagine it, you can manifest it. You can take the photo or image you choose for this spell from a magazine, print it out from a website, or draw it yourself.

Picture of what you desire, or an image that sums up your need
6 or more quartz crystals
1 small white candle

1. Perform this spell on the night of the full moon.
2. Place the image on your altar. While looking at it, visualize yourself enjoying your goal exactly as you wish it to be. Imagine white light surrounding the picture.
3. Place the crystals, one by one, clockwise around the photo. Every time you add a crystal, visualize the light around the photo becoming larger and brighter. Make a complete circle of crystals around the picture, its aura glowing like an orb of light.
4. Light the white candle. Drip some wax onto the photo, and then carefully use the hot wax to make the candle stand upright on the image. Feel the heat from the candle and see the added light it brings to the spell.
5. Holding your hands near the flame where you can feel its heat, say, *Crystal circle, fire and flame, full light of the moon. Manifest (what you need) in my life before the next full moon.*
6. Imagine yourself enjoying your goal while the candle burns all the way down, covering the image in wax.
7. Allow the circle of crystals and wax to stay where they are for one full moon cycle, emanating magical energy to attract what you desire.

It's important to use a small candle for this spell, as a large taper or votive will burn for hours. Small candles, called chime candles, are perfect for spells and are available in many witchcraft shops.

DOUBT-DESTROYER SOAP

Often the biggest obstacle that stands between you and your desires is self-doubt. This feeling dulls the focus and power of your intentions, getting in the way of creating the life you want. This spell is to cleanse the doubt from your mind and spirit, making the path to your true purpose easier to travel.

1 beryl
1 selenite
1 aquamarine
Your favorite soap, bar or liquid
Bowl of rainwater

1. Gather your materials in your sacred space.
2. Empower the beryl, selenite, and aquamarine with the ability to purify negative thoughts.
3. Place your soap on your altar. If it's bar soap, remove the packaging. If it's liquid soap, leave it in the bottle.
4. Place the three crystals around the soap, each one touching it.
5. Dip your fingers in the rainwater and drip in a clockwise circle around the stones, creating a purified, clean space. Visualize the rainwater's cleansing energy filling up the circle and imbuing the soap and crystals with the power of purification.
6. Allow the crystals to sit touching the soap for three days, filling it with their cleansing properties.
7. Once a day for three days, repeat the rainwater circle and the visualization. Your soap is now ready to use.
8. Every time you wash your hands or body, imagine the soap drawing out all your doubts in the form of murky gray blobs of energy. The doubt is pulled to the surface of your physical and energy body and disappears, leaving behind a pure, positive spirit that is open to all the universe has to offer.
9. Use this soap anytime your doubts and negative thoughts are getting in the way of manifesting your magic.

Store this soap in a special place for when you need it. Sometimes the discouraging words of others can cling to you and affect your sense of power. This soap will remove that unwanted energy as well.

CONNECTING TO THE ASTRAL REALM

There's a well-known saying in witchcraft: As above, so below. This means what you create in the astral realm will manifest in your earthly life. The astral realm is where your intentions and visualizations first take form while you are casting spells. This meditation is to create a strong bond between your earthly self and your astral self.

1 oval brown jasper palm stone
1 oval selenite palm stone

1. Choose a quiet place to meditate. Sit with the jasper in your right hand and the selenite in your left hand.
2. Feel the physical differences in the stones; notice each one's weight, temperature, and texture. Notice their distinct vibrations: Jasper is earthy and stable, whereas selenite has an ethereal feel to it.
3. Visualize the jasper growing roots like a tree, spreading into your hand, through your arm, and down your body into the ground. The jasper stone roots you in the physical plane.
4. Visualize the selenite emitting a glowing white light that flows into your hand, up your arm, and bursts out of the crown of your head. This light reaches so far into the sky you cannot see where it ends; the astral realm is infinite.
5. Focus on the roots below you and the light above you. Notice how energy of the two stones merge inside your body, separate but together. Your physical body is of the earth, like the jasper. Your spiritual self is of the astral, like the selenite. Together they create a perfect balance.
6. Allow this energy to flow through you for as long as you are comfortable. Enjoy the feeling. You may become aware of sounds, images, or other sensations. These are the two realms communicating with you.

7.   When you're finished, write down any thoughts or images that came to you during this experience. They may not make sense right now, but the more often you practice this meditation, the more meaningful the information will become.

This meditation aligns your spirit body with your physical body, which creates a sense of purpose and harmony. It should feel extremely relaxing, and you should feel balanced and content afterward.

PSYCHIC FRIENDS

This working involves at least two people. It will help create a psychic bond between the participants, allowing mental messages to be sent over physical distances. You can do this spell with a friend just for fun and then compare your experiences, or with someone you wish to stay connected to from afar by doing this ritual with them before you part.

2 purple candles in holders
2 angelite crystals
2 carving tools for the candles, such as nails or a stylus

1.   Sit facing each other. Place an unlit candle in front of each person, along with an angelite crystal.
2.   Carve your name in your own candle, while your friend carves their name into theirs. You're each putting your own unique vibration into the candles, not only with your names but also with the physical energy you exert in carving them.
3.   Light the candles, set them in the holders, and join hands. Say in unison three times, *A circle of hands, a tie that binds, fire and stone connect our minds*. Release your hands.
4.   Hold your angelite stones to your foreheads, over the third eye. Visualize indigo light pouring from your third eye into the crystal. Say in unison, *Connected to the angelite, my third eye shares my divine sight*.
5.   Place the stones between you so they're touching.
6.   Each hold your purple candle in your right hand. Bring the candles together so that the flames become one over the top of the angelite stones. Say in unison three times, *The flames are one, the crystals are one, our minds are one*.
7.   Blow out the candles.

8. Exchange stones and candles. When you wish to send your friend a psychic message, light the candle with their name on it, hold their angelite, and focus intently on the message you're sending them.

You can do this spell with a group of people if you wish, creating a psychic bond among everyone in the group. Just add more candles and stones, sit in a circle, and repeat the spell.

CRYSTAL ORACLE

You can create your own crystal oracle using this working. You can then consult your oracle whenever you need guidance, answers to specific questions, or just a general sense of what to expect on any given day. Select stones for your oracle that you're familiar with and know the meaning of by sight. Preferably, they should be crystals you have charged under a full moon.

1 candle in a holder
1 stick incense
1 soft cloth for casting the stones
Collection of 10 to 15 different tumbled crystals and stones
1 bag to hold the crystals

1. Sit at your altar or in your sacred space. Light a candle to establish mood and burn some incense. Lay the casting cloth on a flat surface.
2. Holding your bag of crystals in your hands, take some deep, relaxing breaths.
3. Reach into the bag and caress the stones with your fingers while whispering your question out loud.
4. When it feels right, grab several stones and gently release them onto the cloth. There's no need to do this roughly; dropping them from just 3 inches above the cloth is fine.
5. Interpret the stones that have landed on the cloth according to their magical properties. Here are some tips:
   • The stone closest to the center of the cloth is most important. The energy it represents factors strongly into the answer.
   • If two stones are touching, it means two different influences are at play. For example, a rose quartz touching black onyx would mean strife in a relationship.

- If the stones you selected are all similar colors, consider the magical meaning of this color as a message.
- If the same stone keeps showing up for every question you ask, it has a meaningful message for you right now in your life. Meditate with this stone or sleep with it near you to understand its significance.
- If a crystal does something specifically to catch your attention, such as rolling far away, falling off the table, or some other strange behavior, it's sending you a meaningful warning.

In between readings, place your bag of stones on a selenite disk, if possible. Don't forget to charge your oracle crystals under the full moon whenever you can.

AWAKEN AND GROW SPELL

Spiritual awakening is a never-ending process; even the most experienced witches continue to grow, change, and learn as they open up to Spirit throughout their lives. This spell can be performed by both new and experienced witches to encourage spiritual awareness and growth in their magical practice. Bean seeds are hearty and easy to grow year-round indoors, but if you're good at gardening you can use any kind of seeds you like for this spell.

1 empty flowerpot
Purple paint
1 paintbrush
Potting soil
1 amethyst crystal
3 seeds

1. Gather all your materials.
2. On the inside bottom of the pot, paint the word *awake*, along with the image of an eye. Eyes represent spiritual wisdom, protection, and magical power.
3. Fill the pot with soil. Visualize the soil being imbued with the power of the ancient symbol of the all-seeing eye.
4. Place your amethyst crystal before you, and carefully place three seeds so they're either resting on the amethyst or touching it.

5. Visualize the mystical purple aura of the amethyst soaking the seeds. Focus on the life and growth contained in them. Hold both palms above the stone and seeds and say, *Tiny seeds contain all life. The all-seeing eye that knows. Amethyst for awakening. My spirituality grows.*
6. Plant the seeds and the amethyst in the soil.
7. Hold the pot up to the sky and say, *As these seeds germinate, so does my inner knowing. As the leaves open, so does my mind. As the plants reach toward the light, so does my spirit.*
8. Place the plant in a sunny spot where it will thrive. Be sure to nurture the seeds into plants with water and light. You will grow spiritually alongside the plant. In the warm months, move the plant outdoors to complete its life cycle and cleanse the amethyst.

You can take this a step further by only watering your seeds with moon water. Moon water is water that has been left outdoors under the full moon to absorb its power.

PAST LIFE RECALL BRACELET

This wearable charm will help you recall your past lives. Past lives have a large impact on your current incarnation, and unearthing them can provide important knowledge to aid you on your spiritual journey. All the items for this spell can be purchased in craft shops.

Howlite beads (enough to encircle your wrist)
1 candle
1 feather
1 bowl of water
1 rock
Elastic string for beading (1 piece large enough to encircle your wrist)

1. Empower your howlite beads with past-life recall.
2. Gather your items at your altar with a candle in the south, a feather in the east, a bowl of water in the west, and a rock in the north to represent the four elements.
3. Make a tight knot at one end of the elastic and string the beads on from the opposite end. As you do so, repeat the chant *In all I do and all I see, my past lives are revealed to me.*

4. When you've strung the length of the elastic, tie the ends together with a double knot and trim off the excess.
5. Touch your bracelet to the feather. Say, *I invoke the spirits of air to carry lost memories to me on the wind.*
6. Hold the bracelet in the heat of the candle flame. Say, *I invoke the spirits of fire to spark my memories of times long gone.*
7. Touch your bracelet to the water. Say, *I invoke the spirits of water to reveal the undercurrents that move beneath this life.*
8. Touch your bracelet to the stone. Say, *I invoke the spirits of earth to reveal what is buried deep within.*
9. Now, hold the bracelet up to the sky. Say, *I invoke the sacred spirit of life that resides in all things, larger than time and beyond the stars. Reveal to me the infinite cycles of my soul.*
10. Wear your bracelet and be open to the information it reveals.

Evidence of past lives can take the form of dreams, repetitive symbolism in your waking life, fears that you can't explain, or a sudden sense of clarity.

AMMOLITE WITCH BATH

Some witches like to take a ritual bath before magical workings. These baths, which often include oils, herbs, and salt, are meant to clear away the energetic debris of everyday life and imbue the witch with heightened magical powers. This particular bath draws upon the symbolism of ammonite or ammolite, which are spiral fossils of ancient sea creatures.

1 purple candle
3 tablespoons sea salt
3 drops frankincense oil
3 drops sandalwood oil
1 ammolite or ammonite fossil

1. Light the candle to set the mood, turn out the lights, and run a warm bath.
2. Add the sea salt and the oils to the bathwater. With your hand, churn the water in a sweeping clockwise movement, creating the same unending spiral pattern as is in the ammolite.

3. Think about how the spirit of ancient oceans exists in every drop of water on earth. Say, *I welcome the spirits of water to this space to purify and empower me. Reveal the mystical undercurrents, the secret knowledge of the ages, the wisdom of the deepest oceans.* Keep moving the water in a clockwise movement while visualizing it becoming a deep, spiraling vortex of occult secrets.

4. Slip into the bath and relax. Take some deep breaths, inhaling the scented oils and allowing the candlelight to put you in a magical headspace.

5. Bring the ammolite stone to your forehead. Keep your eyes closed. Imagine its spiral formation resonating deep within you. The spiral represents the constant unfolding of life's mysteries. These mysteries are now in you and in the water all around you.

6. Meditate on the spiral and water undulations for about 15 minutes. Feel the dark, mysterious undercurrents of the oceans all around you. Whenever your mind wavers, bring your thoughts back to the spiral.

7. You may discover that you actually experience a spinning feeling. Go deep into this experience and allow yourself to be part of the never-ending spiral of creation.

8. Afterward, dry yourself, drain the bath, and proceed with whatever magical working you had planned.

Ritual baths aren't meant to physically clean the body but are for ritual purposes only. Consider taking a real shower first, so you can fully enjoy a ritual bath for purely spiritual reasons.

SPELL TO REMOVE SADNESS

Turquoise stones are known for absorbing energy, making them perfect for removing unwanted emotions and other vibrations from the physical and astral bodies. This spell is to help someone overcome lingering melancholy, misplaced emotions, or preoccupations. It can also help overcome past events that continue to haunt a person.

1 turquoise stone
1 small black box with a lid

1. Cleanse, charge, and empower your turquoise with the ability to absorb sadness.
2. Sit or lie down comfortably in a place where you will not be disturbed. A bright, sunny place is ideal.
3. Visualize your own aura. If you're in emotional pain, you will see or feel areas that seem murky or dim. Pay attention to where these spots are located.
4. Place the turquoise on each part of your body listed in the following steps while reciting the incantation accompanying each. Visualize any murky energy in that specific part of your body being sucked into the turquoise and held there.
5. Feet: *With this, I remove all sadness from my feet so that I may follow my path in perfect love and perfect trust.*
6. Thighs: *With this, I remove all sadness from my legs so that I may stride into my future with strength and courage.*
7. Belly: *With this, I remove all sadness from the center of my being so that I may manifest all of my desires and know my worth.*
8. Heart: *With this, I remove sadness from my heart so that I may love and be loved without fear or judgment.*
9. Throat: *With this, I remove sadness from my voice so that I may speak my truth freely.*
10. Third eye: *With this, I remove sadness from my third eye so that I may send and receive psychic information with clarity.*

11. Crown of your head: *With this, I remove sadness from my spirit so that I may experience the profound wonder of the universe without doubt.*
12. Hands: *With this, I remove all sadness from my hands so that I may produce joy in all I touch.* Imagine the very last of the murky energy leaving your hands and being absorbed by the turquoise.
13. Place the turquoise in the box and shut the lid. Spend some time enjoying your newly cleansed energy body. You should feel light and hopeful.
14. Bury the turquoise in the ground to heal it, and then empower it under the next full moon to be reused. Dispose of the box.

If you're familiar with the chakra system, you can tweak this spell to reflect it by placing the turquoise on each energy center and envisioning the associated color.

SPELL TO RELEASE THE PAST

This spell will include a piece of aragonite and other natural objects to represent past events that are holding you back from realizing your full potential. This working can be performed when clinging to past relationships or dwelling on old pain. The materials used are sharp, thorny, and dead to represent the negative aspects of the past.

Piece of paper
Pen
Small bits of dead twigs
1 leaf from a thistle or other thorny plant
Sharp stones
1 aragonite crystal

1. Gather your materials at your altar.
2. Write on the paper all the things you want to break free from. Don't hold back. This can be situations, a list of people, or anything you can think of. Lay the paper flat on your altar.
3. Place the dead twigs in the center of the paper. Say, *This is for all the times I felt powerless. I release these feelings.* Visualize the people or situations that made you feel this way and mentally transfer that energy into the twigs.

4. Place the thorny leaf on top of the sticks. Say, *This is for all the pain I have felt. I release these feelings.* Visualize as you did with the twigs.
5. Add the sharp stones to the paper. Say, *This is for all the fear that makes it hard to traverse the present. I release these feelings.* Visualize again.
6. Now the pile of dead plant matter and stones is filled with your past pain, surrounding it with spiky, stormy energy.
7. Place the aragonite crystal on top of the pile and envision it neutralizing that spiky aura, making it fizzle out like water putting out a fire. The glow of the crystal essentially kills the energy you've put into the other objects.
8. Wrap the paper securely all around this mixture.
9. Go to a flowing river or a body of water with lots of movement. Unfold the paper and release the contents into the rushing water. Allow it, and past influences, to be carried away from you forever. Burn or recycle the paper.

You can add any item that represents your past to this spell, as long as it's biodegradable. This spell may bring up some difficult emotions to be released, so be gentle with yourself afterward.

MICA MINDFULNESS MEDITATION

For this meditation, you'll be creating a loving, nurturing physical space in which to practice mindfulness. Mindfulness brings peace and calm by focusing on yourself and your surroundings in the moment, which quiets out-of-control thoughts and eases anxiety. Intentionally creating a loving space and then practicing mindfulness within it can be refreshing and rejuvenating.

1 soft blanket
3 light blue candles
Fresh flowers
Your favorite incense
1 mica crystal

1. Set up a comfortable place to sit or lie down with your blanket and other materials. Have the candles, flowers, and incense where you can see them, along with the mica crystal.
2. Light the candles and incense and make yourself as comfortable as possible.
3. Take five deep breaths and relax.
4. Look deeply at the gentle flames and colorful flowers. Inhale the aroma of your favorite incense. Every time a thought tries to intrude, bring yourself back to just what you can see with your eyes. Notice how the soft shadows dance on the walls, how the flames flicker, and the soothing blue of the candles themselves.
5. Move your attention to the flowers. Appreciate each one, noticing each petal, and how their growth patterns follow sacred geometry.
6. Move your attention to the incense smoke, noticing its mellow undulations in the air and its beautiful scent.
7. Move your attention to the softness of the blanket, how it feels against your skin.
8. Hold your mica crystal over the warmth of the candle flames and allow it to absorb the gentle heat. Pass it through the incense to imbue it with the luxurious scent. Touch it to some of the flowers, to empower it with beauty. Move your attention to how the mica feels in your hand.
9. Try to spend 10 minutes in this state of mindfulness, focusing only on what you see, feel, and smell. When your thoughts wander, bring them back to the present, which is full of beauty and softness.
10. When you're done, blow out the candles. Carry your mica stone with you. Any time you feel scattered, chaotic, or overwhelmed, find a quiet place to hold your mica stone and take deep breaths. It has absorbed the peace of the candles, flowers, and incense. You can invoke those things again when meditating with this stone.

You can replace any of these materials with whatever makes you happy, joyful, and relaxed. Everyone is different, so feel free to add anything to this space that brings you joy and a sense of peace.

SOCIAL MEDIA TALISMAN

Social media can be fun, but it can also have a negative effect on your emotional health, especially if you spend time comparing your life to carefully edited, curated feeds. This spell creates a talisman to protect your self-confidence while navigating social media content. Be mindful of what you're absorbing on social media. Unfollow or block any source that makes you feel bad about yourself.

Peridot ring, worn on the hand you scroll with
Chalice
Moon water
1 small piece fresh or dried valerian root
1 fresh lemon slice

1. Cleanse and empower your ring with the ability to dispel feelings of envy and inadequacy.
2. Gather your materials in a sunny area during a waning moon.
3. Fill the chalice with moon water.
4. Take the valerian root in your hand and hold it in the direct sunlight. Say, *Valerian root that calms the sting, add self-assurance to my ring.* Visualize it absorbing the sun and pulsing with a gentle, healing light. Place it in the chalice.
5. Hold the lemon slice up to the sun, feeling the illumination and bright energy coming from it. Say, *Bright yellow lemon with a bite, filter that which befalls my sight.* Squeeze the lemon slice so the juice goes into the chalice.
6. Now the chalice holds a soothing brew imbued with calm from the valerian, confidence from the sunlight, and optimistic realism from the lemon.
7. Put the peridot ring in the chalice and let it sit in the sun for about an hour.
8. Retrieve your peridot ring from the chalice and wear it. Pour the water into the earth. The ring will help ground you in reality while filtering your impressions of what you consume on social media, protecting your self-confidence and dispelling any feelings of jealousy or inadequacy.

Perform this spell in direct sunlight, if possible, to illuminate the truth and soothe uncertainty. If you don't have a chalice, use a bowl, or any kind of cup. Moon water is water that has been left outdoors under the full moon to absorb its power.

SOCIAL BATTERY CHARGER

Long periods of socializing and sharing energy closely with others can leave you feeling severely drained and in need of alone time. This experience is heightened for those who consider themselves introverts, resulting in extreme discomfort. This spell creates an amulet to help you recharge when you're overwhelmed by social activity, or to act as a general social battery charger for introverts.

> Small pieces of red tourmaline
> Wax paper or tray (optional)
> Translucent oven-bake clay (available at craft stores)
> Copper shavings
> Bits of clear quartz

1. Cleanse, charge, and empower your red tourmaline with social strength and emotional recovery.
2. Gather your materials. You might wish to work on wax paper or a tray, as you'll be using clay.
3. On a day you're feeling healthy, rested, and positive, take a piece of clay about the size of your thumb and knead it with your fingers until it's pliable. While you're kneading the clay, imagine you're sending your current balanced mood through your fingertips into it, filling it with your fully charged battery.
4. Add the bits of red tourmaline and knead them into the clay. Imagine these crystals add another layer of energy to the clay, one of strength and fortitude.
5. Knead the copper filings into the clay, visualizing them amplifying the energy already there.
6. Add your quartz crystals.
7. Mold the clay mixture into the shape of a pyramid with a square bottom. It may not be perfect, and that's okay. Make the best pyramid you can.
8. Bake the pyramid according to the instructions on the package of clay.

9. Carry the pyramid charm with you when you know you're going to be socializing for a long time. When needed, find a quiet spot and rub the charm between your fingers, feeling the magic of the materials combined with the pyramid charging you up like a battery.

The shape of the pyramid amplifies the energy of the red tourmaline, quartz, and copper. This charm can be placed outdoors on the full moon to charge, just as you do your other crystals.

PEACEFUL-ATMOSPHERE SPELL

This spell incorporates a blue lace agate to promote peace and serenity in the home. It can be performed to bring a sense of tranquility to your space, whether you live alone or with other people. You can also carry the stone with you after the spell to bring that sense of tranquility with you everywhere you go. This spell should be done during a waxing moon.

Pin or other sharp object for carving a candle
1 light blue candle in a holder
1 blue lace agate

1. Gather your materials in your sacred space. Cast a circle, if you wish.
2. With the pin, carve the word *peace* on the candle from top to bottom. Now, spend a moment holding the blue lace agate and feeling its calm, loving energy.
3. Gently rub the stone all over the surface of the blue candle. Imagine the crystal is bathing the candle and the carved words in soothing blue light.
4. Visualize your desired outcome, harmony in your home, exactly as you wish it to be. Put the candle in the holder and place the blue lace agate at its base.
5. Light the candle and hold your hands near the flame to feel its nurturing warmth. Say, *Warming fire and loving stone, bring peace and calm into my home. Spread your gentle spirits here to keep calm and contentment near.* Lower your hands.

6. Imagine the candle is sending out a sphere of pale blue light that grows to fill your home. Visualize the glow permeating your surroundings, then spreading outward into each room. It flows into every corner and crack. Allow the light to grow in your mind until it's spilling out the windows and doors.

7. You can let the candle burn down all at once or light it for a few moments each day while visualizing your intention. When the candle is gone, place the blue lace agate somewhere in the home where it can continue to send out its peaceful energy.

This spell is especially useful after a stressful period in life, following an illness, or when there have been arguments between members of the household.

CRYSTAL GRID FOR HEALTH

This crystal grid attracts healthy energy for your physical body into your space. It can be made to help alleviate illness in the home or to generally attract vibrant healthy energy. Strong physical energy can help dispel lethargy and contribute to overall well-being. You'll be using Metatron's Cube grid for this spell. You can simplify what you put on the piece of paper by just drawing a symbol of wellness such as the sun, a blooming flower, or a human form with outstretched arms.

Small piece of paper with your health intentions written on it
Metatron's Cube template
1 large tiger iron stone
6 small quartz points
6 carnelians
Wand or athame

1. Find a spot to make your grid that won't be disturbed by people or pets.
2. While you draw your health symbol or write your specific intention on the paper, visualize yourself and everyone you live with as physically healthy and feeling well, however that looks for you and them. If you're concerned about a specific illness, visualize it being managed successfully.
3. Place your paper in the center circle of the Metatron's Cube grid and place the tiger iron on top of it. This is your Master Stone. Tiger iron represents physical strength and victory over adversity—including health-related adversity.
4. In the six circles surrounding the tiger iron, place your quartz points, with their points pointing toward the tiger iron. These are your Way Stones.
5. On the six outer circles of the grid, place your carnelians. These are your Desire Stones.
6. Using your wand or athame, trace the pattern of the grid just above the crystals. Be sure to connect all the lines while visualizing your goal.

7. Spend a moment feeling the vibrant, healthy strength coming from the grid, and imagine its energy filling the area all around it.

You can place this grid in the bedroom of anyone who is feeling a need for greater physical wellness. Be sure to seek professional medical attention along with making this crystal grid when it comes to health issues.

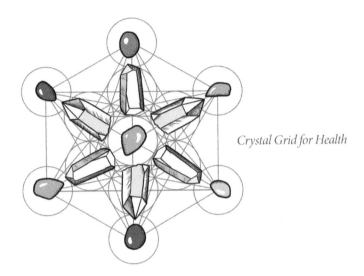

Crystal Grid for Health

WITCH BOTTLE FOR WELLNESS

Witch bottles, or spell bottles, have been used in witchcraft since ancient times. A witch bottle is a collection of meaningful magical items aligned with an intention that are sealed in a bottle. In this one, the lilac brings harmony, bay leaves are for inner strength, and rosemary promotes physical wellness. This witch bottle can be kept in the home to bring wellness and health to your space.

   1 incense stick
   Glass bottle with a lid or stopper
   1 sunstone
   1 red agate
   1 citrine
   Flowers or leaves from a lilac tree
   Dried rosemary
   3 bay leaves
   1 lock of your hair

1. Assemble all your materials on your altar.
2. Light the incense. Use the smoke to make circles around your gathered ingredients, moving clockwise as if you're stirring a big pot of soup. As you create circle after circle, chant repeatedly, *Health. Wellness. Strength. Body, mind, and soul.* As you chant, a rhythm will emerge. Combine the rhythm and the motion of the circle until you sense that energy has been raised.
3. Put the incense aside in a holder. Place the items into the jar one by one. As you do, spend a moment with each one visualizing its purpose and power before putting it in. Add your lock of hair last.
4. Cap or cork the jar.
5. Place the jar in direct sunlight for one day, allowing it to soak up the vital rays of the sun.
6. Then, keep the jar somewhere in your home where you will be able to see it and feel its energy at least once a day. Visualize it sending out a bright beacon of positive orange energy every time you are near it.
7. Once a month or so, recharge it by putting it in the direct sunlight.

Witch bottles can be made for almost any magical goal. Get creative with ingredients suited for love, prosperity, protection, and other objectives. Collect bottles that you find aesthetically pleasing to have on hand for making these simple magical amulets.

IOLITE HABIT BREAKER

These days there are innumerable unhealthy ways to numb ourselves from life's uncomfortable realities. Bad habits involving substances, technology, or other destructive, repetitive behaviors can destroy us mentally and physically. This spell is for when you find yourself engaging in a habit that is bad for your health and would like to break the cycle.

2 jars with lids
1 teaspoon white sugar
Handful of coarse ashes from a fire, or pebbles
1 cup water
1 square of cheesecloth
1 rubber band
1 iolite egg

1. Gather your materials on your altar.
2. Place the sugar in one jar and the handful of ashes or pebbles in the other jar.
3. Add the cup of water to the jar containing the pebbles or ashes. The water represents your mind and body, and the dirt represents the bad habit. Put the lid on the jar and shake it. Observe how the dirt and refuse contaminate the water, making it murky and hard to see through. Visualize the habit that is interfering with your wellness.
4. Place the cheesecloth over the jar with the sugar in it and secure it with the rubber band.
5. Gently and carefully pour the dirty water through the cheesecloth into the jar with the sugar, straining out all the debris. Clean water now fills that jar.
6. Shake up the clean water with the sugar. Visualize the sugar infusing it with sweetness and peace. This clean, sweet water is your new life, free of the bad habit.
7. Place the iolite egg in this clean water and let it sit for 1 hour, then remove it.
8. Hold the iolite in both hands. The egg shape symbolizes new life and fresh beginnings. The iolite itself will empower you to overcome that which holds you back and keep you strong and forging ahead.
9. Meditate regularly with the egg in one hand and then the other, visualizing your new, healthy self growing. Dispose of the water and other materials.

This spell is best performed during a waning moon. You may wish to sleep with this egg under your pillow as well, to absorb its vibrant, hopeful energy.

GREEN JASPER TEA

This spell combines the medicinal properties of herbal tea with the magical power of green jasper. Drink this tea daily, or any time you need a dose of wellness. This is an all-purpose health tea, but if you're knowledgeable about herbs you can create your own, or simply perform this rite with your favorite bagged tea. Remember to speak to a doctor before drinking herbal tea, as it can interfere with medications and complicate or worsen certain conditions.

Dried herbs chosen for your specific needs; here are
some suggestions:

- Chamomile: rest
- Echinacea: boost the immune system
- Elderflower: boost antioxidants
- Ginger: intestinal issues
- Hibiscus: high blood pressure
- Peppermint: digestion
- Rose hips: inflammation
- Sage: promote brain health

1 green jasper

1. Put your dried herbs in a cup or a tea ball.
2. Boil enough water to fill a cup or a small teapot.
3. When the water is boiling, pour it into the cup. Allow the herbs to
   steep for 10 minutes.
4. Add the jasper to the tea.
5. If you take milk or sugar, add it now.
6. Hold your hands around your mug and feel the warmth of the
   tea. Close your eyes and inhale the scent. Imagine the heat is a
   warm glow of healthy energy, the steam coming off of it waves of
   healing vibrations.
7. Remove the green jasper.
8. Drink your tea in a quiet place where you can meditate and stay
   mindful. Feel it entering your stomach and then spreading its
   goodness throughout your veins. Imagine its warmth confronting
   whatever health issue you are dealing with and softly washing
   it away.
9. Visualize yourself cleansed and empowered from the inside out.

A bonus to this spell is that if you're drinking the tea loose rather than using
a tea ball, you can read your own tea leaves afterward.

BOJI STONES BALANCING MEDITATION

Every day we're faced with the challenge of achieving a healthy balance between work and play, activity and rest, thinking and doing. A pair of boji stones is perfect for finding balance in all aspects of life. The feminine stone is receptive, whereas the masculine stone is active. Try to sense this difference as you hold them.

> 1 black candle
> 1 white candle
> 1 feminine boji stone
> 1 masculine boji stone

1. Sit at your altar. Light both the candles. They may be opposite in color, but note how their flames exude equal amounts of power.
2. Hold the feminine boji stone in one hand, the masculine stone in the other.
3. Allow the vibration of the stones to enter you. Feel the energy flowing into the feminine boji, into your hand, up your arm, and through your head. At the same time, feel the masculine boji pulling energy from your head, down your right arm, and out through your palm. The two stones work together in a constant balanced dance of receiving and sending, giving and taking, creating a perfect flow of energy in and out of your body.
4. Sit for as long as you can, feeling the boji stones pulling positive energy in and then expressing positive energy out. If you sense some kind of blockage, try switching hands.
5. If your mind starts to wander, bring your focus back to the stones and the giving and receiving energy that flows through your body. This river of energy running through your system balances your mind, cleanses your body, and empowers your spirit.
6. When you're done meditating, place a boji at the base of each candle—whichever one feels right—and blow out the flames.

Anytime you're feeling overwhelmed by either giving or taking, have been absorbing excessive amounts of other people's energy, or exerting too much of your own, boji stone meditation is a soothing respite.

HEALING WITCH DOLL

Clay, wax, and cloth dolls are a familiar sight in witchcraft, but are often misunderstood and portrayed in a negative light. The truth is, witch dolls can be made for any purpose and are excellent for healing. This spell is to send intense healing energy to someone who needs it, using a witch doll.

Air-drying clay
1 small object belonging to the person, or a piece of their hair
1 small clear quartz crystal empowered with healing energy
1 soft white cloth

1. Ask for permission from the person targeted by this spell before proceeding.
2. Perform this spell at your altar during the waxing or full moon.
3. Form a human shape out of the clay. Visualize the person as you form the doll. It helps to chant their name while you work, being sure to keep their face in your mind. Give the doll their hairstyle, body shape, and general appearance.
4. Knead their hair or a small object belonging to them into the clay while you work. This will ensure a link between them and the doll.
5. When the doll is complete, set it before you on your altar.
6. Take the quartz crystal in your hand. Hold it up to the moon, preferably where you can see the moonlight through the crystal. Say, *Gentle moon, loving light, I call you through this stone, send healing power through this crystal, that (name) will be cured of what ails them.*
7. Firmly press the crystal into the clay figure, on the part of the body affected by the illness. The crystal is bringing a milky beacon of healing moonlight directly into the doll while simultaneously sending healing energy into the person it represents.
8. Let the doll dry. Wrap it in soft white cloth and keep it hidden until the illness passes.

Quartz is known as the master healer, and that's why it's used in this spell. However, you can use more specific crystals if you have an understanding of their various healing powers.

SAMHAIN: MESSAGES FROM THE DEAD

This ceremony is to welcome benevolent spirits of the dead into your space and receive their messages. The human skull is believed to create a conduit between the dead and the living. The dead are all-knowing and can respectfully be contacted in many ways, including through a crystal skull.

1 (9-foot piece) black string with the ends tied together
Athame
1 glass wine or juice
1 cup graveyard dirt
1 quartz crystal skull
1 coin

1. Gather your materials, outdoors if possible, after dark.
2. Lay the string in a circle on the ground with your materials inside it. Stand inside the circle, facing east. Using your athame or your index finger, trace the perimeter of the circle clockwise while saying, *This magic circle protects me during this working. By the power of the elements, no unwanted spirits can cross this boundary.* Finish in the east.
3. Sit within the circle. Set the glass of wine across from you, as if you're facing someone.

4. Between yourself and the glass of wine, make a small mound with the graveyard dirt. Place the crystal skull upon it.

5. Hold the glass of wine up to the night sky. Say, *Spirits of the mighty dead, I invite you to my circle. With love and respect, I honor you.* Pour the wine into the ground as an offering.

6. Pick the skull up in both hands and look into its face. Say, *Beloved ancestors and benevolent strangers, I invite you to come through this crystal and speak to me. I am open to hearing your messages and accepting your guidance.*

7. Gaze into the crystal skull. Allow yourself to fully relax. You may wish to close your eyes and receive mental images from the spirits. Pay attention to what you feel, hear, see, and smell. All of these impressions can be messages from the dead.

8. When you are in a receptive state, you will understand what all these impressions mean, especially if you're adept at meditation. Otherwise write your impressions down for later interpretation.

9. When you're finished, place the coin on the graveyard dirt and say, *Dearest dead, thank you for your wisdom and connection.*

10. Remove the circle by again tracing it with your athame, going counterclockwise this time.

11. Remove all the materials except the coin and the graveyard dirt; leave those behind.

Graveyard dirt is exactly that—dirt taken respectfully from a graveyard. While collecting graveyard dirt, be sure to leave behind offerings to the dead, such as crystals, coins, or flowers.

YULE: YULE TREE CRYSTALS

The tradition of decorating an evergreen tree on the winter solstice goes back thousands of years. Bringing a green, lively tree into the house and decking it with joyful colorful objects has always been done to symbolize hope and the awaited return of the sun during the cold, dark months. Here are some crystal suggestions to string on the tree as ornaments to represent your wishes for the future.

These crystals empowered with the following intentions:

- **Amethyst: psychic ability**
- **Black tourmaline: protection**
- **Carnelian: creativity**
- **Citrine: personal power**
- **Clear quartz: spiritual awareness**
- **Red jasper: material stability**
- **Rose quartz: love**
- **Sodalite: communication**

Spool of thin wire
Yule tree

1. Wrap each crystal securely with wire, finishing with a loop for hanging.
2. When you're decorating your Yule tree with all your traditional decorations, add the crystals last. Place them around the top of the tree, just below where you'd put a star or angel. The tree is a pyramid shape, and its greatest concentration of power is at its tip.
3. As you hang each crystal on the tree, say the following affirmations:

AMETHYST: *I trust my psychic senses.*

BLACK TOURMALINE: *My home, loved ones, and I are protected and safe.*

CARNELIAN: *The fire of creativity burns brightly within me.*

CITRINE: *I manifest everything I need.*

CLEAR QUARTZ: *My spirituality grows and knows no bounds.*

RED JASPER: *I have everything I need to live comfortably.*

ROSE QUARTZ: *I am loved, and I love others.*

SODALITE: *I speak my authentic truth.*

4. Visualize the energy of the rainbow of crystals gathering at the tip of the tree and shooting beautiful multicolored light out of the top and into the universe to manifest.

You can store your Yule crystals with your other holiday decorations and repeat this ritual every year. Remember to cleanse and charge them during the December full moon.

IMBOLC: KNOT MAGIC CEREMONY

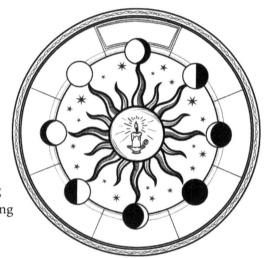

Imbolc anticipates the warmth and light of the coming spring. This ritual harnesses the power of Imbolc and combines it with knot magic. Knot magic is done by anchoring energy into a knot or braid, thus tying it to your own spirit.

1 red candle
1 white candle
1 black candle
1 quartz pyramid
1 (1-inch) piece red string
1 (1-inch) piece white string
1 (1-inch) piece black string

1. On the morning of Imbolc, gather your materials at your altar.
2. Place the candles in a triangle around the pyramid.
3. Light your candles and say, *On this day, I light the fires and ask the earth to wake. This is the dawn of growth and form, as day begins to break.*
4. Notice how the flames reflect in the surface of the pyramid. Visualize the fiery energy of the candles streaming into the base of the pyramid and being drawn up through its point.

5. Touch the red string to the red candle and say, *Fires burn bright, bring health to my life.* Visualize yourself achieving one of your health goals.
6. Touch the white string to the white candle. Say, *Fires burn bright, bring spirituality to my life.* Visualize yourself having an active, fulfilling spiritual practice.
7. Touch the black string to the black candle. Say, *Fires burn bright, bring protection to my life.* Visualize yourself being shielded from all harm in the coming months.
8. Tie the three pieces of string together at one end. This binds the separate energies. Now, braid the three strings. As you do so, chant, *The earth is waking, the light is coming, these three wishes start to grow.*
9. When you've braided to the ends of the strings, knot them together so they won't unravel. Slide the braid beneath the crystal pyramid. The pyramid is amplifying not only the sacred fires of Imbolc, but your wishes as well.

This spell is general enough that you can change the wishes to match your own intentions. Red, black, and white are the traditional colors of Imbolc, but you may use any colors you like.

OSTARA/SPRING EQUINOX: OSTARA GIFTS OF DIVINATION

This magic combines divination with gift giving. You can include any crystals and stones you wish, as long as you know their meanings. This working will divine what energies are coming up for the summer and fall months for your friends. Even non-witchy people will enjoy this meaningful spring gift.

Strips of colorful paper
Pen
Plastic hollow eggs or an eco-friendly alternative
Various crystals (one for each egg)
Fabric bag

1. On each strip of paper, write something such as *Your fortune-telling crystal for this spring is (crystal name), the stone of (meaning)*. So, for example, *Your fortune-telling crystal for this spring is pyrite, the stone of prosperity*. Remember to keep it positive. (Below are some suggestions. Refer to chapter 3 of this book for more ideas.)
   - Amethyst: spirituality
   - Bloodstone: opportunity
   - Blue lace agate: peace
   - Carnelian: passion
   - Citrine: joy
   - Jasper: stability
   - Quartz: personal power
   - Rose quartz: friendship
2. Roll up the strips of paper. Place each one inside an egg along with the matching crystal. Make as many as you would like to give as gifts. If you have a lot of people on your list, some of them may receive the same stone.
3. Lay all your eggs out in the sun. Visualize them absorbing the hopeful, rejuvenating essence of spring as it awakens all around them. Say, *On this sacred day, I ask the sun, the earth, and the power of the equinox to fill these eggs with hope, joy, and blessings for those who open them.*
4. Put all the eggs in a bag.
5. Approach each person and have them pull an egg out of the bag. When they open it, they will receive their springtime fortune.

If you can't hand them out in person, you can mail the eggs to people you care about or drop them off in their mailboxes. These eggs all carry a positive message of hope and perfectly fit the optimistic meaning of the spring equinox.

BELTANE/MAY DAY: DEW AND FIRE RITUAL

In this ritual, the sunstone represents action and the active pole in nature, and the moonstone represents introspection and the receptive pole. Unifying these opposites to create new beginnings is what Beltane is all about. Appropriate goals for May Day are love, attraction, fertility, and conception. These goals can be physical, emotional, or spiritual. You will need to perform this ritual in an outdoor space.

1 moonstone
1 sunstone
Trowel for digging
Assortment of wildflowers that you gather beforehand

1. The morning dew on Beltane is thought to be especially magical. Go outdoors at dawn and touch your moonstone to the moisture that has gathered on the ground. While you do this, empower your moonstone with the fertile, creative side of nature.
2. As the sun comes up, bring your sunstone up to absorb the bright new rays. Empower the sunstone with the vital, dynamic side of nature.
3. Find a quiet spot to gather your materials. Inhale the scent and warmth of the new day. Using your trowel, dig a small hole in the earth, the right size to bury both stones. This hole represents the womb, where new life grows.
4. Place your hands inside the hole and feel the cool, grounding energy of the earth. Say, *Nurturing earth, loving mother energy, I ask you to act as a healthful vessel in which my plans and ideas grow.*
5. Hold the sunstone in your right hand and the moonstone in your left. Spend a moment feeling their opposite but equal energy.

Slowly bring them together until they're touching. Visualize a huge spark of power exploding outward at their union. Say, *Sun and moon, fire and water, thought and form, unite. Together we create the whole.*

6. Carefully lower them into the hole in the ground, making sure they're touching.
7. Pack the earth over the top of them. Place the flowers in a small circle surrounding the space as you say, *My dreams and actions come together to germinate safely in the womb of the earth.*
8. Leave the space, knowing it's done.

Growth begins in darkness. Your intentions will continue to develop and manifest over time, just as a seed begins its life underground.

LITHA/SUMMER SOLSTICE: HONORING THE FLOWERS

This is the longest day of the year. The sun is at its zenith and the flowers bask in its light, with their fully bloomed faces turned toward it in celebration. Harnessing the joyous energy of flowers is an excellent way to celebrate the solstice. You can perform this spell in your own garden or anywhere that flowers grow. The crystals listed here are associated with joy, beauty, and expression, just like the flowers.

Some or all of the following stones: cat's-eye, rose quartz, chrysanthemum stone, peacock ore, topaz, clear quartz, citrine, labradorite, opal
Bowl or basket to hold the crystals
All-natural fertilizer or very healthy soil from compost
1 incense stick
Box or bag

1. At noon on the solstice, when the sun is at its highest, place your crystals in the bowl. Cover them with the natural fertilizer and gently mix them together. As you do, visualize your crystals becoming imbued with the fertile energy of the rich soil.
2. Take your bowl of stones and your incense to a place where there are lots of flowers. The meaning of different flowers could be a book all its own, but in this case, you can think of their collective energy as expressions of happiness.
3. Light your incense. Hold the crystals up to the sky. Say, *On this brightest of days, at the brightest hour, I empower these crystals to honor the flowers.*
4. Approach the nearest flower(s) and place a crystal near its roots, along with a dash of fertilizer. Using the incense like a wand, make a circle of smoke around the flower(s) while feeling happiness in your heart.
5. Repeat this step with the rest of your stones, with all the flowers you can find until you've used up your crystals.
6. Lie down on the ground in the full sun, if possible, meditating on how the sun is making the earth bloom and flower, just as it's doing for your own body and aura. Visualize flowers blooming all over you. They represent your goals and wishes coming to fruition.
7. Afterward, gather up your crystals and put them back in the bowl, being sure to send a message of thanks to each of the flowers as you retrieve your stones. Leave the compost behind.
8. Store these crystals in their own special box or bag to keep the flower energy in them safe.

Between now and the next summer solstice, you can draw on these crystals for the joyous, bountiful, blooming energy of summer flowers. Doing so can add power to spells and be useful in meditation when you're feeling down.

LUGHNASADH: GRATITUDE FOR THE EARTH RITUAL

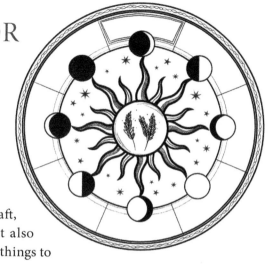

Lughnasadh is traditionally the grain harvest, a time for expressing gratitude to the earth and sun for all that they've produced. This ritual is a simple ceremony of thanks to honor the earth. In modern witchcraft, the earth element means food, but also money, home, and safety, which are things to consider when doing this working.

> Piece of paper
> Pen
> Handful of dried corn kernels or seeds
> Heatproof dish
> Lighter
> 1 crystal associated with love for the earth, such as fuchsite, brown jasper, ruby, green tourmaline, or unakite

1. Write a list of all the things you have harvested between Imbolc and the present. This may be literal, such as herbs for using in magic or food from your garden. It can also be the modern equivalent, such as money, property, or a job.
2. Now, take your dried corn or seeds, and for each item on the list hold a kernel of corn up to the sun. Say, *I am thankful to the elements for (item from list)*. Place the kernel in your heatproof dish. Repeat this step with each kernel until you've finished the list.
3. Roll up the paper and light it on fire, being sure to catch the ashes in the heatproof dish that holds the seeds. The ashes imbue the seeds with your feelings of gratitude.
4. Place your chosen crystal on top of the ashes. Take the dish outdoors either to your own yard or to a wooded area.

5. Say, *Water and air, earth and sun, the growing season is almost done. I thank you for all that I have, all that I've gained, and all that's to come.*
6. Place the seeds and ashes on the ground, with the crystal in the center.
7. The crystal will remain there as a token of your thanks, eventually disappearing into the earth. Wildlife will gather up the seeds or kernels and eat them, integrating your message of thanks back into the great cycle of nature.

You will not be keeping this crystal, as it's being given as an offering of thanks. It can be difficult to part with a favored stone, but consider it a gift to Spirit.

MABON/FALL EQUINOX: WELCOMING THE DARKNESS

The Wheel of the Year is cycling toward the dark months, and it's time to start looking inward. Darkness is often erroneously associated with negative things, but it's important to comprehend its role in nature and in our lives as a precursor to growth. This ceremony will help you understand this as the nights begin to lengthen.

3 black candles
Small mirror
Black paint
Paintbrush

A variety of black crystals; some suggestions are:

- Black obsidian: surviving change
- Black onyx: transforming negative emotions into something useful
- Black tourmaline: shielding
- Dark smoky quartz: navigating emotions of loss and ending
- Jet: becoming wise from experience

1. Gather your materials at your altar after dark on the fall equinox.
2. Light the candles and look at your reflection in the small mirror. Think about what you'd like to let go of over the cold months. This can be anything at all that you feel is holding you back in some way. Whisper your intention out loud into the mirror. Say, *On this pivotal night that marks the return of the darkness, I send that which I no longer need into the great cauldron to be reinvented. I want to change (your intention) for the greater good. So mote it be.*
3. Paint over the mirror's surface with black paint, sealing in your desires.
4. As the paint dries, meditate on letting go of those things that hold you back.
5. When the paint is dry, place your collection of black crystals on the dark surface of the mirror. Their energy protects and seals over what you've decided to give over to the darkness for rebirth.
6. Keep the mirror with the stones on it on a windowsill in your home. Keep them free from dust. Come spring, you should have overcome the issues you whispered into the mirror.

Mabon marks the beginning of the cold part of the year, a time of introspection, rest, and change. This charm will help you see the benefits of its cleansing and banishing symbolism and learn that it's actually a time of renewal and growth.

RESOURCES

BOOKS FOR WITCHES

Alexander, Skye. *The Modern Guide to Witchcraft: Your Complete Guide to Witches, Covens, and Spells.* **Avon, MA: Adams Media, 2014.**
A modern, relevant view on learning witchcraft today.

Illes, Judika. *Encyclopedia of 5,000 Spells: The Ultimate Reference Book for the Magical Arts.* **New York: HarperCollins, 2011.**
A crash course on witchcraft in general, with spells for almost every purpose.

Lipp, Deborah. *Magical Power for Beginners: How to Raise & Send Energy for Spells that Work.* **Woodbury, MN: Llewellyn Publications, 2017.**
Everything you need to know about the relationship between energy and witchcraft.

BOOKS ABOUT CRYSTALS

Cunningham, Scott. *Cunningham's Encyclopedia of Crystal, Gem & Metal Magic.* **Woodbury, MN: Llewellyn Publications, 2002.**
This book is specifically geared toward magical practitioners and witches who work with stones.

Hall, Judy. *The Crystal Bible: A Definitive Guide to Crystals.* **Iola, WI: Krause Publications, 2003.**
The healing and metaphysical properties of many crystals, including unusual and rare ones, are explained in this book.

CRYSTAL RESOURCES

GeologyIn.com

This site lists traveling gem shows throughout the United States. Gem shows are excellent for sourcing crystals of all kinds and give you an opportunity to talk to the vendors about the stones.

Minerals.net

A complete guide to minerals, crystals, and gems.

WITCHCRAFT SUPPLIES

Etsy.com

On this website you'll find hundreds of vendors who are knowledgeable magical practitioners, selling all kinds of handmade witchcraft items.

SacredMists.com

In operation since the 1980s, this shop has a delightfully overwhelming inventory. They have everything a witch could possibly need.

WhiteMoonWitchcraft.com

This online shop sells handcrafted kits, altar tools, jewelry, and personalized made-to-order witchcraft items. As a small business, they craft and curate every one of their products with loving attention.

INDEX

A

Agate, 27, 35, 109, 136
  black agate, 72, 99
  blue lace agate, 48, 72, 133–134, 147
  fire agate, 33, 72
  moss agate, 22, 72, 93
  in protection amulet, 104–105
Alexandrite, 72
Altars, 17, 35, 80, 96, 102
  altar crystals, 22, 27, 31, 42, 48, 57, 83
  Doubt-Destroyer Soap spell,
    placing soap on altar for, 119
  Healing Witch Doll, setting
    upon altar, 141
  images and photos placed
    on altar, 36, 118
  Pentacle Crystal Grid,
    building on altar, 105
  pentacle disks, setting on altar, 10, 16
  quartz tower, placing on altar
    to strengthen rituals, 64
  sea gods and goddesses, beryl
    representing on altar, 45
Amazonite, 35, 72
Amber, 5, 35, 41, 56
Amethyst, 35, 42, 50, 104–105,
  123–124, 144, 147
Ametrine, 40, 42, 50, 72
Ammolite Shell, 73, 125–126
Amulets, 23, 54, 82
  Body, Mind, and Soul Protection
    Amulet, 104–105
  Crystal Prosperity Amulet, 96–97
  flint protection amulet, 76
  green jasper amulet for
    health and balance, 78
  in jewelry form, 26, 29

  lodestone relationship amulet, 111
  mother of pearl, adding to amulets, 81
  Social Battery Charger amulet, 132
  in Surprise Treasure Spell, 93
  witch bottles as magical amulets, 137
Angelite, 73, 121–122
Apache tears, 73
Apatite, 73
Aquamarine, 27, 36, 43, 47, 60, 100, 119
Aragonite, 36, 49, 73, 128, 129
Astral realm, connecting to, 120–121
Aventurine, 22, 27, 35, 44
Azurite, 70, 73

B

Beltane/May Day, 33, 148–149
Beryl, 45, 47, 102–103, 119
Bloodstone, 35, 74, 115, 147
Blue Jasper, 78
Body, Mind, and Soul Protection
  Amulet, 104–105
Bronzite, 74

C

Calcite, 33, 46
Candle magic
  black candle use, 102,
    140, 145, 146, 152
  blue candles for rituals
    and spells, 129, 133
  color of candles, importance
    in spell work, 22
  golden candle in Crystal
    Prosperity Amulet, 96–97

Candle magic (*continued*)
  magic work, lighting candles for
    atmosphere, 17, 122, 125
  meditation, use of candles
    during, 129–130
  Prosperity Candle, 95–96
  Psychic Friends spell, role
    of candles in, 121
  red candles for rituals and
    spells, 107, 116, 145, 146
  white candle use, 9, 16, 100,
    104, 118, 140, 145, 146
Carnelian, 27, 35, 147
  creativity, as empowering, 144
  in Crystal Grid for Health, 135–136
  describing, 47
  Yule/Winter solstice, laying
    out during, 33
Cat's eye, 67, 74, 149
Celestite, 36, 48, 55
Chakras
  Crown Chakra, 42, 45, 46,
    48, 49, 56, 60, 64, 65
  Heart Chakra, 44, 52, 54, 59, 63
  Root Chakra, 40, 52, 55, 56, 61, 62, 68
  Sacral Chakra, 41, 47, 49, 60, 66
  Solar Plexus Chakra, 41, 45,
    50, 53, 60, 63, 66, 67
  Spell to Remove Sadness,
    implementing chakras into, 128
  Third Eye Chakra, 42, 48,
    51, 57, 58, 67, 69
  Throat Chakra, 43, 48, 51, 58, 68, 69
Chalcedony, 49, 67, 104–105
Chrysocolla, 74
Chrysoprase, 75, 116
Citrine, 66, 147, 149
  amethyst, working well with, 42
  fake citrine, distinguishing
    from natural citrine, 50

in Money-Attraction Charm, 92
personal power, citrine
  associated with, 144
sunstone, working well with, 66
in Witch Bottle for Wellness, 136
Yule, laying out during, 33
Color magic, 22–23, 95, 123
Coral, 75
Creativity Candle Spell, 116
Crystal magic
  altar crystals, 22, 27, 31, 42, 48, 57, 83
  broken and lost crystals, 36–37
  care and cleansing of, 14–15
  charging crystals, 14–17
  crystal balls, 24–25, 28
  crystal grids, 29–30, 97–98
  crystal skulls, 25, 142–143
  crystal tools, 28–29
  empowering crystals, 17–18
  formation of crystals, 4–5, 6
  healing and maintenance of, 13–14
  integration of crystals into
    witchcraft, 8, 12, 34–36
  journal, dedicating to sacred
    crystal work, 10
  parting with a favorite stone, 152
  shape impact on magical
    workings, 23–24
  sourcing considerations, 11
  wearing of crystals, 26–27
  Yule Tree crystals, 143–145
Crystal Prosperity Amulet ritual, 96
Crystal Threshold Guardians, 100–101

D

Danburite, 40, 75
Desert Rose, 75
Diamond, 55, 62, 75, 87
Dioptase, 76

Divination
    Crystal Oracle, 122–123
    crystals, divination enhanced
        by, 24, 31, 77, 82
    divination crystals, charging
        under new moon, 34
    divination tools, pairing
        crystals with, 35, 42
    scrying, crystals used for, 28, 45, 61
    symbolism in divination, 96
Doubt-Destroyer Soap, 119

E

Emerald, 52, 76
Epidote, 76

F

Flint, 49, 76, 105–106
Flowers, 98, 135, 143
    in Dew and Fire ritual, 148–149
    Flower of Life grid for love, 112–113
    Honoring the Flowers spell, 149–150
    in House-Cleansing/-Blessing
        Spray, 101–102
    Mica Mindfulness Meditation,
        fresh flowers in, 129–130
    Rose Quartz Attraction Spell,
        rose petals use in, 107–108
    in Witch Bottle for Wellness, 136
Fluorite, 36, 51, 76–77, 101
Fossilized organic materials, 5, 41, 56, 125
Fuchsite, 77, 151

G

Garnet, 27, 33, 52, 60, 112
Gems, 12, 28, 35, 156

Gemstones, 5, 6
Girasol, 77
Golden Quartz, 83
Graveyard dirt, 142–143
Green jasper, 27, 78

H

Healing Witch Doll, 141–142
Hematite, 24, 36, 53, 66
Herbs, 8, 29, 101
    in Ammolite Witch Bath, 125–126
    charging of crystals, herbs used for, 17
    eyebright use in conjunction
        with malachite, 117
    fuchsite as boosting the
        efficacy of herbs, 77
    in Green Jasper tea, 138–139
    green tourmaline, working
        well with, 86
    in Lughnasadh ritual, 151
    in Prosperity Candle spell, 95–96
    Prosperity Grid, adding to, 98
    in Prosperity Powder, 94
    smoke, cleansing with, 14
Howlite, 27, 52, 61, 69, 78, 124

I

Iceland Spar, 78
Imbolc (February 1), 33, 145–146, 151
Incense
    cleansing of crystals in
        incense smoke, 9, 14
    Crystal Oracle, burning
        incense during, 122
    in Curse-Reversal Spell, 103–104
    in Honoring the Flowers
        spell, 149–150

Incense (*continued*)
    in Mica Mindfulness
        Meditation, 129–130
    in money-attraction charm, 92
    in Witch Bottle for
        Wellness, 136–137
Intuition, 23, 27, 81
    beryl, intuitive channels
        opened through, 45
    crystal earrings as enhancing, 26
    crystal grids, laying out
        intuitively, 98
    intuitive attraction to
        certain crystals, 6, 22
    Pisces intuition, crystals
        helping to maintain, 36
    Super Seven stone, increasing
        intuition with, 85
Iolite, 78, 137–138

J

Jade, 5, 35, 54, 97, 98, 109
Jasper
    brown jasper, 27, 34, 65, 78, 120, 151
    magical properties of, 55, 147
    pink jasper, 109
    red jasper, 35, 79, 144
    yellow jasper, 66, 79
Jet, 36, 41, 56, 57, 82, 153
Jewelry, 51, 72, 110
    amber jewelry piece, wearing
        only during spell casting, 41
    amethyst as commonly found
        in magical jewelry, 42
    amulet jewelry, 26, 29
    gemstone use in jewelry, 5
    jade jewelry, suggestions
        for wearing, 54

labradorite jewelry,
    recommended use of, 57
talismans disguised as jewelry, 131
tourmaline jewelry, wearing for
    spiritual protection, 68

K

Knot magic, 145–146
Kunzite, 36, 79, 100
Kyanite, 36, 51, 65, 79

L

Labradorite, 33, 35, 51, 57, 63, 149
Lapis Lazuli, 5, 27, 35, 51, 58
Larimar, 54, 80, 110
Lava rock, 80
Lepidolite, 33, 68, 80
Litha (Summer solstice), 33–34, 149–150
Lithium quartz, 83
Lodestone/Magnetite, 80, 111
Love-Attracting Elixir, 109–110
Lughnasadh/Lammas (August 1), 34,
    151–152

M

Mabon (Autumn equinox), 34,
    152–153
Malachite, 22, 33, 35, 59, 61, 117
Marble, 69, 80
May Day (May 1), 33, 148–149
Meditation
    Ammolite Witch Bath,
        meditation during, 126
    Boji Stones Balancing
        Meditation, 140–141

carnelian, placing on sacral area during meditation, 47
communication with crystals, meditation enhancing receptivity to, 7
Connecting to the Astral Realm meditation, 120–121
Green Jasper tea, drinking during meditation, 139
incense as inducing a meditative state of mind, 9
malachite charm, using during meditation, 117
meditation routine, adding crystals to, 8, 14, 25, 62, 68, 74, 123, 138, 150
Mica Mindfulness Meditation, 129–130
moonstone, placing on solar plexus during meditation, 60
selenite as an ideal stone for meditation, 65
Spell to Heal a Relationship, meditating prior to performing, 108
Merlinite, 80
Metatron's Cube grid, 135–136
Meteorite, 80
Mica, 43, 66, 68, 81, 129–130
Moldavite, 48, 81
Mookaite jasper, 79
Moon magic, 63, 117, 138
full moon, spells done under, 93, 102, 109, 115, 118
lunar magic, 34–35
moon water, 124, 131
Prosperity Candle spell, starting day after new moon, 95
recharging of crystals in moonlight, 15, 16, 122, 123, 128, 145

selenite as associated with the moon, 65, 75
special tray, placing crystals on for moon baths, 9
waxing moon, spells done during, 92, 107, 110, 133, 141
Moonstone, 27, 35, 42, 43, 57, 60, 148

O

Obsidian
black obsidian, 28, 33, 59, 73, 153
crystal balls, obsidian used for, 24
lava, as forming from, 6, 61
snowflake obsidian, 44, 85
Oils
in Ammolite Witch Bath, 125–126
in Creativity Candle Spell, 116
in Go With the Flow Pumice Spell, 114
oils and brews, 29
patchouli oil, 95
Road-Opener Oil, 115
rose water alternative to rose oil, 102
sacred space, cleansing with essential oil spray, 10
Onyx, 35, 62, 103–104, 122, 153
Opal, 27, 35, 57, 63, 149
Opalite, 60
Ostara/Spring Equinox, 33, 146–147

P

Past Life Recall Bracelet, 124–125
Peacock ore, 57, 81, 149
Pearls, 5, 60, 81
Pentacles, 10, 16, 93, 101, 105–106
Peridot, 35, 81, 131
Petrified wood, 27, 41, 55, 56, 82

Picture jasper, 79

Plants, 29, 72, 86
    ancient plants as embedded
        in amber, 41, 43
    Awaken and Grow spell,
        planting seeds in, 123–124
    blessing sprays as replacing
        smoldering plants, 101–102
    crystals, placing near
        plants, 17, 40, 83
    earth as represented by
        plants on altars, 9
    magical connection to plants,
        fuchsite promoting, 77
    potted plants, adding magical
        powders to, 94
    sage, cleansing sacred space with, 10
    in Spell to Release the Past, 128

Prehnite, 54, 82

Prosperity Powder, 94–95

Pumice, 82, 114

Purpurite, 82

Pyramid power, 25, 132–133, 145–146

Pyrite, 34, 58, 147
    iron pyrite, 35, 53
    in Prosperity Crystal Grid, 97–98
    in Prosperity Powder, 94–95

Q

Quartz, 4, 24, 30, 35, 53
    in All-Purpose Manifestation
        Spell, 118
    amulets, quartz amplifying
        the power of, 23
    blue quartz, 33, 82
    charging crystals, use of quartz in, 16
    clear quartz, 27, 36, 56, 64,
        83, 132, 141, 144, 149
    in Crystal Grid for Health, 135–136
    in Crystal Prosperity Amulet, 96–97
    in Crystal Threshold
        Guardians spell, 100
    green quartz, 83, 95
    in Pentacle Crystal Grid, 105–106
    phantom quartz, 58, 64, 83
    in Prosperity Crystal Grid, 97–98
    quartz crystal skull use in Messages
        From the Dead ceremony, 142
    quartz pyramid in Knot
        Magic Ceremony, 145
    rose quartz, 11, 36, 59, 83, 107,
        109, 112, 122, 144, 147, 149
    smoky quartz, 36, 83, 153
    snow quartz, 52

R

Rainbow crystals, 33, 46, 51,
    60, 68, 77, 87, 101

Rainwater, 101, 119

Rhodochrosite, 33, 84

Rhodonite, 62, 84, 105, 108–109

Rites and Rituals, 10, 56, 68
    Ammolite Witch Bath, taking
        before a ritual, 125–126
    ceremonial rites and
        celebrations, 32–34
    chalice use during witchcraft rites, 28
    Dew and Fire Ritual, 148–149
    Gratitude for the Earth
        Ritual, 151–152
    Green Jasper Tea rite, 138–139
    healing rituals, turquoise
        adding power to, 69
    Knot Magic Ceremony, 145–146
    Messages From the Dead
        rite, 142–143

overused crystals, allowing to
rest before new rituals, 13
Psychic Friends ritual, 121–122
rituals and spells, 31, 48
sapphire use in rituals regarding
legal matters, 84
Welcoming the Darkness
ceremony, 152–153
Ruby, 27, 34, 52, 84, 151

S

Sabbats, 32–33
Sacred geometry, 29–30, 106, 130
Sage, 10, 14, 17, 94, 101–102, 139
Samhain (October 31), 33, 142–143
Sapphire, 71, 84
Sardonyx, 84
Seed of Life grid, 97–98
Selenite, 27, 48, 68, 119, 123
Cancer, selenite as well-suited to, 35
cleansing power of, 10, 15
in Connecting to the Astral
Realm meditation, 120
in Crystal Threshold
Guardians setup, 100
moon, as associated with, 65, 75
Serpentine, 45, 84
Social battery charger, 132–133
Social media talisman, 131–132
Sodalite, 27, 36, 85, 144
Soul Mate Spell, 110–111
Spell casting, 18, 63, 86
amber as an amplifier of
spells, 41
aquamarine use in emotional
clarity spells, 43
attraction spells, crystals
used in, 52, 55, 80

fluorite use in studying
and exam spells, 51
legal system spells, crystals
used for, 67, 74
malachite use for spells bringing
life-altering changes, 59
moonstone, choosing for
love spells, 60
peace and harmony spells,
stones suited to, 73, 78, 81
spinel, employing for
breakup spells, 85
success and prosperity spells,
crystals matched with, 47, 75, 87
Spell work, 9, 22, 37
cleansing and reuse of crystals
for spells, 11, 13–14
crystal points, directing
energy through, 23, 24
enhancing of spell results, 8, 50
gemstones, including in spells, 6
gossip-preventing spells,
stones added to, 45, 84
money spells, crystals
included in, 44, 53
Prosperity Candle, renewing
intention when burning, 95–96
protection spells, crystals
associated with, 61, 62
rituals and spells, 31, 48
self-expression and communication
spells, reinforcing, 26
"so mote it be," ending spells
with, 97, 107, 153
Spinel, 59, 85
Spirit Quartz, 83
Stones, 80, 114, 120
Boji stones, 74, 140
chrysanthemum stone, 34, 74, 149

Stones (*continued*)

Desire Stones, 30, 98, 106, 112, 136

hag stones, 34, 77

home-protection stones, 99–100

Master Stones, 30, 69,
97–98, 105, 112, 136

mining of healing stones,
ethical impact of, 11

palm stones, 25, 120

rocks and stones, properties of, 5

Spell to Release the Past, sharp
stones used in, 128

stone spirits, 1, 6, 7, 14

Way Stones, 30, 98, 106, 112, 136

Sugilite, 85

Sun magic

citrine as encapsulating the
power of the sun, 50

cleansing of crystals
with sunlight, 57

Lughnasadh, expressing gratitude
to the sun during, 151–152

Ostara eggs, laying out
in the sun, 147

Road-Opener oil, setting in
sun for three days, 115

Social Media Talisman, creating
in sunny area, 131

Spell to Remove Sadness, doing
in a sunny place, 127

Summer solstice, honoring
the sun during, 149–150

sun baths for crystals, 13, 47

sunlight, charging crystals with, 16

sunrise of Beltane as magical, 148

tigereye as containing sun energy, 67

Witch Bottle for Wellness, placing
in sun for one day, 137

Sunstone, 27, 34, 66

crystals working well with, 43, 69

in Dew and Fire Ritual, 148–149

Leo, as well-suited for, 35

Litha, choosing sunstone to
celebrate the day with, 34

in Witch Bottle for Wellness, 136–137

Super Seven, 47, 85

T

Tarot cards, 36, 42

Teas and brews

essential oil alternatives to
brews, 102

Green Jasper Tea spell, 138–139

mugwort tea, 17

oils and brews, 29

Social Media Talisman brew, 131

tea leaves, reading of, 96, 139

Tiger Iron, 44, 85, 135–136

Tigereye, 34, 36, 53, 67, 94–95

Topaz, 34, 50, 67, 85–86, 149

Tourmaline

beryl, working well with, 45

black tourmaline, 65, 68,
86, 105–106, 144, 153

green tourmaline, 33, 68, 86, 151

Libras, tourmaline as a
good fit for, 35

purple tourmaline, 58, 68, 86

red tourmaline, 63, 68, 87, 132–133

Turquoise, 36, 69, 127–128

U

Unakite, 27, 34, 41, 87, 151

Wheel of the Year, 32, 34, 152

Witchcraft, 8, 40, 57

  as above/so below as the
    witch's motto, 75, 120

  candle magic in, 95, 118

  color meanings in witchcraft, 23

  crystal tools used for, 28–29

  earth element in modern
    witchcraft, 151

  gemstone use in witchcraft
    practices, 6

  green tourmaline as perfect for, 86

  pentacle as a sacred symbol of, 10, 105

  witch bottles, assembling, 136–137

  witchcraft books, keeping
    fluorite near, 51

Yule/Winter Solstice, 33, 143–145

Zircon, 87

Zodiac signs, 35–36

ABOUT THE AUTHOR

Eliza Mabelle has been practicing witchcraft since childhood and has an especially strong affinity for stone spirits and crystals. Eliza's practice is intuitive and solitary, with a strong focus on plants, animals, and the elements. In addition to working with crystals, she's especially fond of sigil magic and herb magic. When she's not up to something witchy, she can be found reading, writing, and making art.